EASY AIR FRYER

EASY AIR FRYER

Susanna Unsworth

SEVEN DIALS

First published in Great Britain in 2023 by Seven Dials,
an imprint of The Orion Publishing Group Ltd
Carmelite House, 50 Victoria Embankment
London EC4Y 0DZ

An Hachette UK Company

1 3 5 7 9 10 8 6 4 2

A CIP catalogue record for this book is
available from the British Library.

ISBN (Hardback) 978 1 3996 1403 0
ISBN (eBook) 978 1 3996 1404 7

Printed and bound in Italy

FSC
www.fsc.org

MIX
Paper from
responsible sources
FSC® C104740

www.orionbooks.co.uk

Commissioning Editor: George Brooker
Art Director: Helen Ewing
Photographer: Jo Sidey
Props Stylist: Faye Wears
Food Stylist: Susanna Unsworth
Head of Production: Katie Horrocks

Imperial and metric measurements have been given in all recipes.
Use one set of measurements only and not a mixture of both.

Contents

Introduction

The recipes in this book are designed to make the most out of your air fryer, whether it's a big or small model, whether you've just bought your first or you're an air fryer veteran on the hunt for new recipe ideas.

Think of an air fryer as a small oven that evenly circulates air around food, cooking it more quickly and using less energy than a conventional oven. For many people, they have become a kitchen staple, mostly because they save so much time and effort (and money) when preparing food.

It's well known that air fryers can cook deep-fried foods with far less oil, but they're capable of a lot more than that!

This book will give you delicious recipes well beyond deep-fried food. You will find new, interesting and diverse ways of cooking using your air fryer, as well as – of course – some air (deep-) fried delights!

Equipment

Air fryers come in various sizes and configurations. Some do run hotter than others, so be prepared to slightly adapt timings and temperature settings when necessary.

Some air fryers have a basket with a section beneath, allowing for two separate components to be cooked in unison. A number of recipes in this book make use of both sections, to save cooking time. If your air fryer does not have two sections, then use your judgement in preparing the separate elements of the recipe one after the other.

For some recipes, you will also need some extra pieces of equipment:

- bottle of spray oil
- paper air fryer liners
- round tin, about 19cm (7½ inches) in diameter
- round baking dish, about 19cm (7½ inches) in diameter
- square baking dish, about 19 × 19cm (7½ × 7½ inches)
- cupcake tin to fit your air fryer (usually round or square and with 7–12 moulds)
- muffin tin to fit your air fryer (usually round or square and with 7–12 moulds)
- meat thermometer

Tips

Having a bottle of spray oil is essential when cooking certain foods in an air fryer, as spraying, rather than drizzling, allows you to coat the food more evenly. For example, food that is coated in breadcrumbs will only become golden on those areas that have been sprayed with oil. In this book, where a spray oil is needed, it is listed in the ingredients section.

Paper air fryer liners do the same job as baking parchment (parchment paper), preventing food from sticking to the cookware, but are made specifically for use in air fryers. Holes in air fryer liners allow air to circulate more freely around the food than baking parchment does. If you don't have air fryer liners, cut holes into regular sheets of baking parchment.

A meat thermometer is a handy tool for confidently measuring the temperature of food, especially meat and fish. If, like me, you're after that perfect medium-rare steak, then you'll make great use of it!

Do not preheat air fryers with aluminium (aluminum) foil or baking parchment inside. The fan could blow them into the top heating element and cause a fire hazard.

BREAKFASTS

Sausage & Egg Breakfast Muffin

Recreate everyone's favourite breakfast at home. With an air fryer, these are quick and fuss-free.

4 sausages
1 teaspoon vegetable oil
2 eggs
2 English muffins
1 tablespoon butter
2 American cheese slices
hot sauce, to serve
   (optional)

1 Preheat the air fryer to 180°C (350°F) for 4 minutes.

2 Remove the skins from the sausages and shape the sausage meat into 2 round patties, similar in size to the muffins. Place the patties into the air fryer and cook for 10 minutes.

3 Meanwhile, oil 2 ramekins and crack an egg into each. Cover the ramekins with some foil, making sure the foil tucks under the ramekins to hold it down. Flip the sausage patties over, then add the egg ramekins to the air fryer alongside the patties and cook for another 5 minutes.

4 Toast and butter the muffins.

5 Remove the egg ramekins and sausage patties from the air fryer. Lay 1 cheese slice on each sausage patty so the cheese gently melts in the residual heat. Carefully run a small, sharp knife around the edge of the ramekins and remove the eggs.

6 Build your muffins: place the sausage patties on the muffin bases first, followed by the eggs. Splash over hot sauce, if you like, and top with the muffin lids.

Hash Browns with Maple Bacon & Avocado

Cooking bacon in an air fryer is a revelation, ensuring perfectly crispy bacon with less fat.

4 bacon rashers (slices)
450g (1lb) floury (starchy) potatoes
1 egg
½ teaspoon baking powder
25g (1oz) plain (all-purpose) flour
½ teaspoon salt
3 teaspoons maple syrup
olive oil, or vegetable oil, for spraying
1 avocado, thinly sliced
5g (1 teaspoon) finely chopped chives
pepper

1 Preheat the air fryer to 190°C (375°F) for 4 minutes. Put the bacon rashers in the air fryer and cook for 8 minutes.

2 Meanwhile, grate the potatoes on the coarse side of a box grater, place into a clean tea towel (dish towel) and squeeze out the liquid.

3 In a medium-sized bowl, whisk together the egg, baking powder, flour and salt until smooth. Add the grated potato to the bowl and stir with a wooden spoon until well combined.

4 Remove the bacon from the air fryer, brush with the maple syrup and set aside. Leave the air fryer on.

5 Line the air fryer with an air fryer liner or baking parchment (parchment paper) that has been pierced with holes and spoon in the potato mix to make 4 hash browns, flattening each one down with the back of your spoon. Spray over a little oil and cook for 7 minutes.

6 Flip the hash browns over, brush or spray over a little more oil and cook for another 7 minutes until golden.

7 Serve the hash browns with the maple bacon, with the avocado on the side, topped with a sprinkle of chives and a good grind of pepper.

Soft-Boiled Eggs with Asparagus

These can be served with toast soldiers instead of asparagus spears; simply add slices of bread to the air fryer at the same temperature for a minute on each side.

250g (9oz) asparagus spears, woody ends snapped off
1 tablespoon extra virgin olive oil, plus extra to serve
4 eggs
salt and pepper

1 Preheat the air fryer to 180°C (350°F) for 4 minutes.

2 Put the asparagus spears into a medium-sized bowl and drizzle over the olive oil. Add salt and black pepper.

3 Place the eggs and asparagus into the air fryer and cook for 7 minutes. The asparagus spears may need 1–2 minutes more, depending on their thickness. They are ready when a sharp knife will pierce the thickest spear with no resistance, but be careful not to overcook them.

4 Plate up the asparagus and crack open the tops of the eggs. Drizzle some more olive oil over the asparagus and give everything a good grind of pepper, then serve.

Spinach & Goat's Cheese Frittata

This simple baked egg dish is delicious and quick to make in the air fryer. You can swap out the spinach for any leafy green.

vegetable oil, olive oil or butter, for the dish

100g (3½oz) spinach

5 eggs

4 tablespoons milk

2 tablespoons roughly chopped dill

2 tablespoons finely chopped chives

25g (1oz) soft goat's cheese (vegetarian, if needed)

salt and pepper

1 Oil or butter a baking dish measuring about 19cm (7½ inches) square that fits in your air fryer, then line it with baking parchment (parchment paper). This doesn't have to be neat!

2 Boil a kettle, place the spinach in a colander and pour over the boiling water to wilt it. Set aside to cool.

3 Preheat the air fryer to 170°C (340°F) for 4 minutes.

4 In a medium-sized bowl, beat together the eggs, milk, dill and chives. Add a large pinch of salt and a generous grind of pepper. Pour the mixture into the baking dish. Squeeze the water out of the spinach and spread it over the egg mixture, then crumble the goat's cheese on top.

5 Cook for 20–25 minutes until the egg is set. To check, insert a skewer: if it comes out clean, the frittata is ready.

Granola

Easy and healthy, you can make this using whatever combination of nuts, seeds and dried fruit you have in your cupboard. This will keep in an airtight container for up to two weeks.

**Makes enough to last
1 week / 7 portions**

150g (5½oz) rolled oats
100g (3½oz) mixed nuts
   (walnuts, pistachios,
   almonds)
30g (1oz) mixed seeds
   (sesame, pumpkin,
   sunflower)
1 teaspoon ground
   cardamom seeds
1 teaspoon ground
   cinnamon
60ml (4 tablespoons)
   maple syrup
2 tablespoons vegetable
   oil
2 tablespoons coconut
   flakes
1 tablespoon desiccated
   coconut
1 tablespoon dried
   cranberries
2 tablespoons raisins
finely grated zest of
   1 orange

1 Preheat the air fryer to 140°C (275°F) for 4 minutes. In a large bowl, mix together the first 7 ingredients.

2 Line the air fryer with an air fryer liner or baking parchment (parchment paper) that has been pierced with holes and spread out the granola mix in a single layer as best you can. Cook for around 20 minutes, stirring every 5 minutes.

3 After 20 minutes, mix in the coconut flakes and desiccated coconut. Cook for another 5 minutes until golden but not too dark. It will harden as it cools.

4 Remove from the air fryer and mix in the cranberries, raisins and orange zest. Leave to cool, then store in an airtight container.

Giant Pancake

This giant pancake is the perfect sharing breakfast: simply slice up and serve. You could leave out the blackberries and serve with crispy bacon for a savoury breakfast.

2 eggs
1 tablespoon caster
  (superfine) sugar
140ml (4½fl oz) milk
80g (2¾oz) plain
  (all-purpose) flour
1 teaspoon vanilla paste
¼ teaspoon fine salt

TO SERVE

icing (confectioner's)
  sugar
maple syrup
a few blackberries

1 Line the base of a round tin that fits in the air fryer, around 19cm (7½ inches) in diameter with baking parchment (parchment paper). Preheat the air fryer to 190°C (375°F) for 4 minutes.

2 Crack the eggs into a medium-sized bowl and add the sugar. Whisk together using electric beaters until frothy, then add the milk, flour, vanilla paste and salt and whisk again until smooth. Pour the mixture into the prepared tin and put it into the air fryer.

3 Cook for 15 minutes, until the mix is set and golden on top. To test if it's ready, insert a skewer: if it comes out clean, it is done.

4 Remove the pancake from the tin, then dust with icing sugar, drizzle over a little maple syrup and scatter over a few blackberries to serve.

Parmesan Baked Eggs

A perfect indulgent Sunday breakfast treat. The combination of oozy egg yolk, double cream and sharp Parmesan works wonders.

2 tablespoons butter, plus extra for the ramekins

2 eggs

4 tablespoons double (heavy) cream

1½ teaspoons Parmesan cheese (vegetarian, if needed), finely grated, plus extra to finish

2 sourdough bread slices

½ garlic clove

salt and pepper

1 teaspoon finely chopped chives (optional)

1 Preheat the air fryer to 180°C (350°F) for 4 minutes.

2 Butter 2 ramekins and crack an egg into each. Put 2 tablespoons of cream into each ramekin, scatter over the Parmesan, sprinkle over a little salt and give them both a grind of pepper. Cover the ramekins with some foil, making sure the foil tucks under the ramekins to hold it down.

3 Place into the air fryer and cook for about 5 minutes. The egg white should be set and bubbling, but the yolk still runny.

4 Meanwhile, toast the sourdough bread, then rub it with the cut side of the garlic clove. Spread with the 2 tablespoons of butter and cut the toast into soldiers.

5 Serve the eggs in their ramekins with the garlic soldiers on the side, grating over some extra Parmesan and sprinkling with chopped chives, if you like.

Herby Scones with Sun-Dried Tomatoes & Feta

These scones are a great way to make use of leftover herbs. Chives, thyme or parsley would also work well here.

250g (9oz) self-raising (self-rising) flour, plus extra for dusting

1 teaspoon baking powder

¼ teaspoon fine salt

1 teaspoon sweet paprika

60g (2¼oz) butter, chilled and chopped

70g (2½oz) feta cheese (vegetarian, if needed)

75g (2¾oz) sun-dried tomatoes, finely chopped

2 tablespoons finely chopped sage leaves

1 tablespoon finely chopped oregano leaves

1 tablespoon finely chopped rosemary

90ml (6 tablespoons) milk, plus extra for brushing

1 Sift the flour, baking powder, salt and paprika into a large bowl and mix well. Add the butter and rub it in with your fingertips until it resembles breadcrumbs. Crumble in the feta, add the tomatoes and herbs and combine until everything looks well distributed. Make a well in the centre, add the milk and mix with a wooden spoon, then use your hands to carefully work the mixture into a dough.

2 Once you have a smooth dough, roll out to a thickness of 2cm (¾ inch), using a little extra flour on the counter to help you. Preheat the air fryer to 170°C (340°F) for 4 minutes.

3 Press an 8cm (3¼ inch) round cutter into the dough to make 5–6 scones. You can re-roll the excess to get some extra scones.

4 Line the air fryer with an air fryer liner or baking parchment (parchment paper) that has been pierced with holes. Place the scones on the parchment and brush the tops with a little milk, avoiding the sides, as this will affect the rise.

5 Cook for around 15 minutes, until risen and golden in colour. Leave to cool on a wire rack. Serve with butter, if you like. These will keep in an airtight container for up to 4 days.

Posh Beans on Toast

With a quick raid of the kitchen cupboard, a simple beans on toast can be rustled up in no time. If you don't have haricot or cannellini beans, try using chickpeas or butter beans, which work just as well.

½ red onion, chopped

1 teaspoon extra virgin olive oil

1 garlic clove, finely grated

½ teaspoon ground cumin

½ teaspoon sweet paprika

400g (14oz) can chopped tomatoes

400g (14oz) can haricot or cannellini beans (white beans), rinsed and drained

2 sourdough bread slices

1 tablespoon sherry vinegar

1 tablespoon roughly chopped flat-leaf parsley leaves

salt and pepper

1 Preheat the air fryer to 180°C (350°F) for 4 minutes. Either put the onion in a baking dish that fits in the air fryer, or use the section underneath the basket if your air fryer has one. Drizzle over the oil and add a pinch of salt, then cook for 5 minutes.

2 Add the garlic and spices to the onion and cook for 3 more minutes, then add the chopped tomatoes and beans and cook for a further 15 minutes until the sauce is thick and reduced.

3 Meanwhile, toast the bread.

4 When the sauce is thick and reduced, add the sherry vinegar, season well with salt and pepper and stir in the parsley. Serve the beans over the toast.

Sweetcorn Fritters with Black Bean Salsa

These are a delicious crowd-pleaser. Serve them as part of a feast, or with a fried egg if you're having them for brunch.

FOR THE FRITTERS

45g (1½oz) plain (all-purpose) flour
1 teaspoon smoked paprika
1 egg
1 tablespoon milk
150g (5½oz) sweetcorn, defrosted if frozen
2 spring onions (scallions), thinly sliced
olive oil, or vegetable oil, for spraying
salt and pepper

FOR THE SALSA

200g (7oz) cherry tomatoes, some halved, others quartered
½ red chilli (chile), deseeded and finely chopped
½ avocado, chopped into small chunks
100g (3½oz) canned black beans, rinsed and drained
2 tablespoons roughly chopped coriander (cilantro) leaves
juice of 1 lime
2 tablespoons extra virgin olive oil

1　Preheat the air fryer to 200°C (400°F) for 4 minutes.

2　Put the flour and paprika into a medium-sized bowl. Crack in the egg, pour over the milk and whisk well until smooth. Add the sweetcorn and spring onions, and season well with salt and pepper. Mix together with a spoon. It should look wet, but firm enough to hold together.

3　Line the air fryer with an air fryer liner or baking parchment (parchment paper) that has been pierced with holes. Spoon in the sweetcorn mix, 1 large tablespoon at a time, to make 6 fritters. Gently smooth over each fritter with the back of the spoon. Spray each fritter with some oil and cook for 6 minutes. Flip the fritters over, then spray them with a little more oil and cook for a further 6 minutes until golden brown and crispy.

4　Meanwhile, in a medium-sized bowl, mix together all the ingredients for the salsa. Season generously with salt and pepper, then set aside.

5　Serve the salsa alongside the fritters.

French Toast with Orange & Figs

If your brioche is slightly stale here, then even better. If you don't have figs, serve this with berries or strawberries instead.

2 eggs
40ml (1½fl oz) double (heavy) cream
1 teaspoon vanilla extract
finely grated zest of 1 orange, plus 1 tablespoon orange juice
2 thick brioche slices
olive oil, or vegetable oil, for spraying
4 tablespoons maple syrup
icing (confectioner's) sugar, for dusting
2 figs, quartered

1 Preheat the air fryer to 180°C (350°F) for 4 minutes.

2 In a shallow dish, whisk together the eggs, cream, vanilla extract and orange zest. Place the brioche slices into the mix, and soak for 1 minute on each side.

3 Line the air fryer with an air fryer liner or baking parchment (parchment paper) that has been pierced with holes. Take the brioche slices out of the batter and place on the parchment, spacing out the slices as well as you can. Spray with a little oil and cook for 6 minutes.

4 Flip the brioche slices over, then spray with a little more oil and cook for a further 6 minutes until golden in colour.

5 Meanwhile, mix together the maple syrup and orange juice.

6 To serve, transfer the brioche slices to plates, pour over the maple-orange syrup, dust with icing sugar and arrange the figs on the side.

Parma Ham Turnovers

These make for an impressive breakfast and can be easily put together. If you don't have Parma ham, use whatever ham you have, or go without to make them vegetarian.

1 × 320g (11½oz) sheet ready-rolled puff pastry
3 tablespoons crème fraîche
1 tablespoon Dijon mustard
6 Parma ham slices
100g (3½oz) Cheddar cheese, grated
1 egg, lightly beaten

1 Preheat the air fryer to 180°C (350°F) for 4 minutes.

2 Unroll the pastry sheet and cut it into 6 equal squares. In a small bowl, mix together the crème fraîche and mustard.

3 With a spoon, spread the mustard mix on to each pastry square, spreading it in a line starting from one corner and running diagonally to the opposite corner. Lay a piece of Parma ham over this, then sprinkle over the cheese.

4 Pick up a corner that has no mixture on it and fold into the middle, then repeat with the opposite corner. Repeat to fill and form 6 turnovers.

5 Brush the pastry with some beaten egg and place into the air fryer basket. You may have to do this in batches.

6 Cook for 12 minutes, until risen and golden.

SNACKS

Courgette Pakoras with Coriander Chutney

The spices used here give these pakoras a vibrant flavour. These are perfect for sharing, or to have all to yourself! You could leave out the coriander chutney and simply serve with some mango chutney.

FOR THE PAKORAS

1 large courgette (zucchini), about 250g (9oz) total weight, grated
½ red onion, grated
1 tablespoon garam masala
½ teaspoon ground coriander
¼ teaspoon ground turmeric
pinch of chilli (chile) powder
70g (2½oz) gram flour
olive oil, or vegetable oil, for spraying
salt

FOR THE CORIANDER CHUTNEY

60g (2¼oz) coriander (cilantro), plus extra to serve
1 green chilli (chile), deseeded
2 tablespoons Greek yogurt
juice of 1 lemon
1 teaspoon sugar

1 Preheat the air fryer to 180°C (350°F) for 4 minutes.

2 Put the courgette and red onion in a medium-sized bowl, add the spices and gram flour, and season well with salt. Give this a mix with a wooden spoon. The liquid from the courgette should be enough to bind it together, but add a splash of water if it seems too dry.

3 Line the air fryer with an air fryer liner or baking parchment (parchment paper) that has been pierced with holes. Spoon the mix on to the parchment, making 5–6 individual pakoras. The mix might be quite sticky, so use another spoon to help you scrape it off. Using the back of a spoon, smooth down the pakoras. Spray with a little oil and cook for 8 minutes, then turn the pakoras over, spray with a little more oil and cook for a further 5 minutes until golden in colour.

4 Meanwhile, put all the ingredients for the chutney into a blender along with a pinch of salt, and blitz until smooth. If it looks too thick, add a splash of water to loosen.

5 Serve the pakoras with the chutney and sprinkle over some extra coriander leaves.

Parmesan Chicken Wings

These wings are seriously addictive … you may want to double up on this recipe. They're epic dipped in blue cheese dressing, or a spicy Buffalo sauce.

1 tablespoon baking powder
1 teaspoon garlic powder
1 tablespoon dried oregano
400g (14oz) chicken wings, wing tips trimmed, halved through the joint
30g (1oz) butter
1 garlic clove, finely grated
20g (¾oz) Parmesan cheese, finely grated, plus extra for serving
finely grated zest of 1 lemon
5g (1 teaspoon) finely chopped chives
olive oil, or vegetable oil, for spraying
salt and pepper

1 Preheat the air fryer to 200°C (400°F) for 4 minutes.

2 Put the baking powder, garlic powder, oregano and some salt into a medium-sized bowl and mix together. Add the wings and toss to coat in the baking powder mix. Place the wings in the air fryer, skin-side up and in a single layer. Spray liberally with oil, then cook for around 15 minutes until crispy and golden.

3 Meanwhile, put the butter and grated garlic in a small bowl and melt for 40 seconds in the microwave. Transfer this mixture to a medium-sized bowl and add the Parmesan and lemon zest. When the wings are ready, toss them through the Parmesan mix.

4 Serve on a plate, sprinkled with chives, extra Parmesan and a good grind of pepper.

'Nduja Croquettes

These spicy air fried delights will be ready in no time using shop-bought ready mash or leftover homemade mash. Swap the 'nduja for harissa paste for an equally punchy vegetarian version.

40g (1½oz) 'nduja
400g (14oz) mashed
  potato
25g (1oz) Gruyère cheese,
  finely grated
25g (1oz) Cheddar
  cheese, finely grated
3 tablespoons plain
  (all-purpose) flour
2 eggs
100g (3½oz) panko
  crumbs
olive oil, or vegetable oil,
  for spraying
salt

1 Place the 'nduja in a small bowl and melt in a microwave for about 15 seconds. Keep an eye on it, as it can burn easily. Once melted, tip it into a large bowl and add the mashed potato, both cheeses and a pinch of salt. Mix together with your hands, then roll into little log shapes, about 40g (1½oz) each. Put them on a tray in a single layer.

2 Put the flour, eggs and panko into 3 separate small, shallow dishes. Season the flour with a pinch of salt and lightly beat the eggs with a fork.

3 Each croquette will have a double panko coating. Place 1 croquette into the flour, shake off the excess, then place into the egg, then into the panko. Place each croquette back into the egg and then the panko. Put them into the fridge on the tray for 10 minutes to firm up.

4 Preheat the air fryer to 180°C (350°F) for 4 minutes.

5 Line the air fryer with an air fryer liner or baking parchment (parchment paper) that has been pierced with holes and put in the croquettes, spacing them out well. Spray liberally with oil and cook for 5 minutes. Turn over, spray over some more oil and cook for another 5 minutes until golden brown.

Courgette Fries

A delicious and irresistibly crunchy alternative to potato fries. These are perfect served with an antipasti spread: get your best cured meats and cheeses, and watch everyone fight over the bowl.

---

3 tablespoons plain (all-purpose) flour

2 eggs

100g (3½oz) panko crumbs

1 courgette (zucchini), cut into 2cm (¾ inch) batons

olive oil, or vegetable oil, for spraying

2 tablespoons finely grated Parmesan cheese (vegetarian, if needed)

salt and pepper

1 Put the flour, eggs and panko into 3 separate small shallow dishes. Season the flour with a pinch of salt and lightly beat the eggs with a fork.

2 Preheat the air fryer to 180°C (350°F) for 4 minutes.

3 Put a courgette baton into the flour, shake off the excess, then place into the egg, then into the panko. Repeat to coat all the courgette batons, putting the coated ones on a baking tray as you go.

4 Line the air fryer with an air fryer liner or baking parchment (parchment paper) that has been pierced with holes. Spread the batons out on the parchment, spray with oil and cook for 7 minutes. Turn over, spray with a little more oil and cook for 7 minutes more, until crispy and golden.

5 Sprinkle over the Parmesan and serve.

Chilli-Feta Corn Riblets

These chilli corn riblets are seriously addictive, and so quick and easy to make in the air fryer. You will need to use a bit of force to cut through the core, so be careful!

---

2 corn cobs
1 teaspoon smoked paprika
1 teaspoon ground cumin
1 teaspoon dried oregano
1 tablespoon extra virgin olive oil
1 red chilli (chile), thinly sliced into rounds
10g (¼oz) coriander (cilantro), leaves picked
30g (1oz) feta cheese (vegetarian, if needed)
salt and pepper

1   Using a sharp knife, trim the ends of the corn. Stand a cob on its end and cut through the core, being very careful and keeping your fingers well away from the blade. Cut each half again through the core to create quarters, or leave as halves if you prefer. Repeat for the other corn cob.

2   Put the riblets into a large bowl and add the paprika, cumin, oregano, oil, a pinch of salt and a grind of pepper, then cook in the microwave for 1 minute to soften slightly.

3   Preheat the air fryer to 180°C (350°F) for 4 minutes. Place the corn into the air fryer and cook for around 20 minutes, until the riblets have curled and the edges are starting to crisp.

4   To serve, arrange on a platter, scatter over the red chilli and coriander, then crumble over the feta.

Tikka Lentil Filo Cigars

These quick filo pastry snacks are so tasty and use only a handful of ingredients.

400g (14oz) can green lentils, drained and rinsed
3 tablespoons tikka masala paste
½ pack filo pastry (phyllo dough), about 3 sheets
about 3 tablespoons vegetable oil
salt
mango chutney, to serve (optional)

1 Put the lentils and tikka masala paste into a medium-sized bowl. Add a generous pinch of salt and stir, then set aside.

2 Cut each filo sheet widthways into 3 strips, brushing each piece all over with a little oil.

3 Preheat the air fryer to 180°C (350°F) for 4 minutes.

4 Take a piece of filo, place it in front of you and spoon a little of the lentil mix in a line along the edge closest to you. Fold over the sides to cover the ends of the line of filling, then roll tightly away from you. The oil you've brushed on should be enough to help the pastry stick together. Repeat to fill and form 9 rolls.

5 Place into the air fryer and brush over a little more oil. Cook for 5 minutes, then turn and cook for another 5 minutes. Serve with mango chutney, if you like.

Loaded Fries

Making chips in the air fryer is so quick and easy, and it's also a great way to use up forgotten, sprouting potatoes. If you fancy good old simple fries, just leave out all the toppings from this recipe.

2 large potatoes, peeled and cut into 2cm (¾ inch) batons
3 teaspoons salt
4 bacon rashers (slices)
½ red onion, thinly sliced
juice of ½ lime
1 tablespoon extra virgin olive oil
2 teaspoons fajita seasoning
30g (1oz) grated mozzarella cheese
30g (1oz) Cheddar cheese, grated
1 green chilli (chile), thinly sliced into rounds
5g (1 teaspoon) finely sliced chives
3 tablespoons soured cream

1　Fill a large bowl with cold water. Add 2½ teaspoons of the salt, along with the potatoes. Put the bowl into the fridge for around 20 minutes.

2　Preheat the air fryer to 190°C (375°F) for 4 minutes. Put the bacon rashers into the air fryer and cook for 8 minutes until crispy, then leave to cool. Reduce the temperature of the air fryer to 170°C (340°F).

3　Put the onion into a small bowl with the lime juice and remaining ½ teaspoon salt. Mix together and set aside to lightly pickle.

4　Line a baking tray with kitchen paper (paper towels), then drain the potato batons and rinse under cold water. Spread them out on the prepared tray and pat them dry. Place the potato batons into a bowl with the oil, give them a mix, then place into the air fryer. Cook for 10 minutes, give them a shake, then increase the heat to 200°C (400°F) for a further 7 minutes.

5　Sprinkle the fajita seasoning over the fries and shake to coat, then tip them on to a tray. Sprinkle over both cheeses, then crumble over the crispy bacon. Top with the chilli, chives, pickled red onion and soured cream, and serve.

Prawn Toasts

You won't believe the crunch you can get on these toasts without the need for buckets of oil. The air fryer ensures they come out perfectly crisp.

3 thick white bread slices
160g (5¾oz) raw king
    prawns (jumbo shrimp)
1 spring onion (scallion),
    roughly chopped, plus
    extra to serve
2cm (¾ inch) piece of
    root ginger, peeled
    and roughly chopped
1 garlic clove, roughly
    chopped
1 teaspoon cornflour
    (corn starch)
1 tablespoon egg white
1 teaspoon soy sauce
1 teaspoon sesame oil
1 teaspoon white sesame
    seeds
crispy chilli oil, to serve
    (optional)

1 Preheat the air fryer to 200°C (400°F) for 4 minutes.

2 Put the bread into the air fryer for 1 minute, then turn over and cook for a further 1 minute until golden and toasted; you may need to do this in batches.

3 Place all the other ingredients except the sesame seeds into a blender and blitz until smooth. Spread the mixture over 1 side of each piece of bread and sprinkle over the sesame seeds.

4 Place back into the air fryer; you may have to do this in batches. Cook for 2 minutes.

5 Slice into triangles and serve with chilli oil and chopped spring onion, if you like.

Gyoza

These impressive crispy dumplings can be made ahead of time and kept in the fridge until you're ready to serve. To make them vegetarian, replace the prawns with a combination of mushrooms and cabbage.

10 gyoza wrappers

olive oil, or vegetable oil, for spraying

FOR THE FILLING

160g (5¾oz) raw peeled prawns (shrimp)

½ red chilli (chile), roughly chopped

1cm (½ inch) piece of root ginger, peeled and roughly chopped

1 garlic clove, roughly chopped

1 spring onion (scallion), roughly chopped

1 teaspoon rice wine vinegar

2 teaspoons soy sauce

1 teaspoon sesame oil

FOR THE DIPPING SAUCE

2 tablespoons crispy chilli oil

2 teaspoons soy sauce

1 teaspoon mirin

2 tablespoons rice wine vinegar

1 Place all the ingredients for the filling into a blender and pulse until the mix comes together but still has some texture to it. If you don't have a blender, just finely chop everything by hand and mix together.

2 Place 1 gyoza wrapper in the palm of your hand. Put 1 heaped teaspoon of the filling mixture into the centre of the wrapper. Lightly dip your other finger into a glass of cold water, then circle around the edge of the wrapper. Bring together the edges of the wrapper, and, starting from one end, pinch together, creating pleats. Repeat to fill and form all the gyoza.

3 Preheat the air fryer to 190°C (375°F) for 4 minutes. Spray both sides of the gyoza liberally with oil, then place into the air fryer. Cook for around 10 minutes, until the gyoza are crispy and golden brown.

4 Meanwhile, whisk together all the ingredients for the dipping sauce.

5 Serve the gyoza with the dipping sauce.

Marmite & Caramelised Onion Toasties

The combination of sweet caramelised onions and salty Marmite gives these toasties a huge depth of flavour.

2 onions, finely sliced
1 tablespoon extra virgin olive oil
25g (1oz) butter
1 teaspoon caster (superfine) sugar
2 teaspoons Marmite (yeast extract)
4 sourdough bread slices
6 Cheddar cheese slices
salt

1 Preheat the air fryer to 150°C (300°F) for 4 minutes.

2 Either put the onions in a baking dish that fits in the air fryer, or use the section underneath the basket if your air fryer has one. Add the oil, 15g (½oz) of the butter and a pinch of salt. Cook for around 15 minutes. Keep checking the onions, giving them a stir now and then. If they are taking on too much colour, reduce the heat slightly and add a splash of water.

3 After 15 minutes, add the sugar and Marmite, then cook for 5 minutes more, until the onions are looking jammy and caramelised.

4 Meanwhile, spread the remaining butter over the bread slices. These will be the outside of your toasts.

5 Lay the cheese slices evenly on the unbuttered sides of 2 of the bread slices. Top with the onions and put the other slices of bread on top, butter-side up. Increase the air fryer temperature to 180°C (350°F).

6 Place the sandwiches into the air fryer basket and cook at 180°C (350°F) for 6 minutes, then turn over and cook for another 6 minutes, until toasted.

Cauliflower Buffalo Bites

Using Buffalo sauce here gives these cauliflower bites a real hot kick. They are a perfect sharing starter; serve them with sticks of celery and cucumber and a ranch dressing.

1 small cauliflower, cut into florets

60g (2¼oz) natural yogurt (plant-based, if needed)

1 teaspoon garlic powder

50g (1¾oz) panko crumbs

olive oil, or vegetable oil, for spraying

3 tablespoons Buffalo sauce

salt

TO SERVE

ranch dressing, to serve (optional)

Celery and cucumber, chopped into batons

1 Preheat the air fryer to 200°C (400°F) for 4 minutes.

2 Place the cauliflower into a medium-sized bowl, then add the yogurt, garlic powder and a pinch of salt. Mix well until fully coated.

3 Place the panko into another medium-sized bowl, then add the cauliflower florets and toss through.

4 Line the air fryer with an air fryer liner or baking parchment (parchment paper) that has been pierced with holes and put the florets into the air fryer. Spray over a little oil and cook for 15 minutes.

5 Pour the Buffalo sauce into a medium-sized bowl. Add the cooked cauliflower and toss to coat, then return it to the air fryer for a further 5 minutes. Serve with ranch dressing, celery and cucumber, if you like.

FRESH & SIMPLE

Charred Corn Salsa Salad

This sweet, zingy, spicy salad is the perfect accompaniment to any Mexican feast. It would work well with Prawn tacos (see page 76).

FOR THE CORN

4 corn cobs
olive oil, or vegetable oil,
   for spraying

FOR THE SALSA

300g (10½oz) vine
   tomatoes, cut into
   large chunks
1 avocado, cut into 2cm
   (¾ inch) pieces
1 spring onion (scallion),
   finely sliced
½ jar roasted red
   peppers, about 225g
   (8oz), cut into thin
   strips
½ red onion, finely sliced
1 red chilli, deseeded and
   finely chopped
juice of 1 lime
15g (½oz) coriander
   (cilantro) leaves
2 tablespoons extra
   virgin olive oil
salt and pepper

1 Preheat the air fryer to 200°C (400°F) for 4 minutes.

2 Place the corn cobs into the air fryer, spray with a little oil and cook for 15 minutes. Turn over, spray with a little more oil, then cook for a further 10 minutes until the corn is browning and charred in places.

3 Meanwhile, put all the salsa ingredients into a medium-sized bowl, season with salt and pepper and mix well.

4 Cut the corn kernels off the cobs, mix into the salsa and serve.

Carrots with Feta

Sweet carrots and tangy feta make a perfect match in terms of flavour. This makes a great accompaniment to a simple roast chicken, but is also delicious served on its own.

FOR THE CARROTS

500g (1lb 2oz) carrots, larger ones halved lengthways
2 garlic cloves, bashed but kept in their skins
1 tablespoon extra virgin olive oil, plus extra to serve
40g (1½oz) butter
1 tablespoon soft dark brown sugar
100g (3½oz) cooked grains, from a pouch
70g (2½oz) strained Greek yogurt
1 tablespoon pistachios, roughly chopped
5g (⅛oz) coriander (cilantro) leaves
5g (⅛oz) flat leaf parsley leaves
2 teaspoons sumac
salt and pepper

FOR THE FETA

100g (3½oz) feta cheese (vegetarian, if needed)
1 tablespoon extra virgin olive oil
finely grated zest of 1 lemon

1 Preheat the air fryer to 170°C (340°F) for 4 minutes. Either place the carrots and garlic in a baking dish that fits in the air fryer, or use the section underneath the basket if your air fryer has one.

2 Drizzle the carrots and garlic with the oil, dot on the butter and sprinkle over the sugar. Season with salt and pepper. Cook for around 15 minutes. Remove the garlic from the air fryer, then increase the temperature to 180°C (350°F) and cook the carrots for a further 10 minutes, until they are tender and blistered in places.

3 Meanwhile, remove the skin from the garlic. Place all the feta ingredients into a small blender, along with the roasted garlic and a pinch of salt. Blitz until smooth.

4 Microwave the grains for 1 minute to warm through.

5 Spread the feta on a platter and place the carrots on top, followed by the grains and pistachios, then scatter over the herbs and sprinkle over the sumac. Finish with a drizzle more olive oil and serve.

Crispy Chickpeas with Broccoli

Crispy chickpeas are a delicious snack on their own, but they also give a wonderful crunch to salads such as this.

100g (3½oz) canned chickpeas, rinsed and drained
1 teaspoon ground cumin
1 teaspoon ground coriander
90g (3¼oz) harissa paste
3 tablespoons extra virgin olive oil
200g (7oz) Tenderstem broccoli (broccolini)
1 red onion, cut into small wedges
100g (3½oz) cherry tomatoes, halved
220g selection mixed sized tomatoes, some quartered, some halved
25g (1oz) flat-leaf parsley leaves
salt and pepper

1 Preheat the air fryer to 200°C (400°F) for 4 minutes. Dry the chickpeas with some kitchen paper (paper towels) and put into a medium-sized bowl. Add the ground spices, along with a generous pinch of salt.

2 Put into the air fryer and cook for 15 minutes, giving them a shake every 5 minutes. Remove and set aside.

3 Meanwhile, in a small bowl, mix together the harissa and olive oil.

4 Either put the broccoli and red onion wedges into a baking dish that fits in the air fryer, or use the section underneath the basket if your air fryer has one. Drizzle over half the harissa oil, mix, then season with salt and pepper. Reduce the air fryer temperature to 180°C (350°F) and cook for 10 minutes.

5 Add the cherry tomatoes to the broccoli and onion, then cook for a further 5 minutes. The broccoli and red onion should be tender and charred in places, and the tomatoes soft but still holding their shape.

6 Arrange the broccoli, onion and cooked tomatoes on a platter. Top with the raw tomatoes, drizzle over the remaining harissa oil, scatter over the parsley and finish with the crispy chickpeas.

Chicken Caesar Salad

The ultimate comfort salad. By cooking the bacon and chicken together, you reduce the time it takes to get this impressive dish ready.

50g (1¾oz) ciabatta, cut into 2cm (¾ inch) pieces

1 tablespoon extra virgin olive oil

2 boneless skin-on chicken thighs, about 100g (3½oz) each

2 bacon rashers

1 Romaine lettuce, larger leaves roughly chopped, smaller leaves left whole

60g (2¼oz) sun-dried tomatoes, roughly chopped

FOR THE DRESSING

70g (2½oz) crème fraîche

30g (1oz) natural yogurt

1 teaspoon Dijon mustard

2 tablespoons extra virgin olive oil

2 anchovy fillets

1 teaspoon white wine vinegar

½ garlic clove

2 tablespoons finely grated Parmesan cheese, plus extra to serve

salt

1 Preheat the air fryer to 200°C (400°F) for 4 minutes.

2 In a small bowl, mix together the ciabatta and oil. Put into the air fryer and cook for around 8 minutes until golden and crispy. Take out and set aside.

3 Reduce the temperature to 180°C (350°F) and put the chicken and bacon into the air fryer basket in a single layer. Spray the chicken with some oil and cook for 7 minutes. Remove the bacon and cook the chicken for a further 8 minutes.

4 Meanwhile, place all the dressing ingredients into a small blender with a small pinch of salt, and blitz until smooth.

5 Cut the cooked chicken into thick slices.

6 Put the salad leaves into a large bowl and drizzle with half the dressing. Crumble in the bacon and add the tomatoes, chicken and croutons. Give everything a toss, then drizzle over the rest of the dressing. Finish with more grated Parmesan and serve.

Salmon Niçoise

Cooking the elements simultaneously makes light work of this salad. You can replace the salmon with a can of tuna, if you like.

200g (7oz) green beans, trimmed

2 tablespoons extra virgin olive oil

2 salmon fillets, around 115g (4oz) each

2 eggs

1 butterhead lettuce, larger leaves torn, smaller leaves left whole

200g (7oz) cherry tomatoes, halved

2 tablespoons pitted black olives, halved

salt and pepper

FOR THE DRESSING

2 tablespoons red wine vinegar

1 teaspoon Dijon mustard

5 tablespoons extra virgin olive oil

1 Preheat the air fryer to 180°C (350°F) for 4 minutes. Place the green beans into a bowl, drizzle over 1 tablespoon of the olive oil, season with a pinch of salt, then mix.

2 Line the air fryer with an air fryer liner or baking parchment (parchment paper) that has been pierced with holes. Place the salmon fillets along with the beans in the basket and rub over the remaining tablespoon of oil. Season with a pinch of salt and grind on a little pepper. Cook for 5 minutes, until the flesh of the salmon is firm and coral pink in colour. Remove the salmon and parchment and set aside, leaving the beans in the air fryer.

3 Put the eggs into the air fryer basket and cook with the beans for 8 minutes.

4 Meanwhile, in a small bowl, whisk together all the ingredients for the dressing, then set aside.

5 Fill a medium-sized bowl with cold water. Plunge the eggs into the cold water and leave for 3 minutes. Peel the eggs and cut in half lengthways.

6 Remove the salmon skin and slice the flesh into large pieces.

7 To serve, arrange the lettuce on a platter followed by the green beans, tomatoes, olives, eggs and salmon. Drizzle over the dressing and give a good grind of pepper, then serve.

Sardines with Marinated Tomatoes

The combination of sweet tomatoes and savoury tapenade make this the ideal summer salad.

60g (2¼oz) sourdough bread, cut in 2cm (¾oz) pieces

2 tablespoons extra virgin olive oil

6 whole sardines, around 75g (2¾oz) each, gutted and cleaned

300g (10½oz) mixed sized tomatoes, some halved, others quartered

10g (¼oz) basil leaves, roughly chopped

salt and pepper

FOR THE TAPENADE

150g (5½oz) pitted black olives

1 teaspoon capers

1 anchovy fillet

20ml (4 teaspoons) extra virgin olive oil

1 teaspoon red wine vinegar

FOR THE DRESSING

3 tablespoons sherry vinegar

5 tablespoons extra virgin olive oil

1 Preheat the air fryer to 200°C (400°F) for 4 minutes.

2 In a small bowl, mix the sourdough with 1 tablespoon of the oil, then put the pieces into the air fryer. Cook for around 8 minutes until the bread starts to turn golden and look crispy. Transfer to a medium-sized bowl.

3 Line the air fryer with an air fryer liner or baking parchment (parchment paper) that has been pierced with holes, then add the sardines. Season with some salt and drizzle over the remaining 1 tablespoon of oil. Reduce the air fryer temperature to 180°C (350°F) and cook for 9 minutes.

4 Meanwhile, in a small bowl, whisk together the dressing ingredients. Season generously with salt and pepper. Mix half the dressing into the bowl of croutons, then add the tomatoes and mix well. Leave to marinate.

5 Put the ingredients for the tapenade into a small blender, then pulse-blend, keeping some texture to it (the same consistency as pesto).

6 Serve the sardines over the marinated tomatoes and croutons. Spoon over some tapenade, drizzle over the remaining dressing and scatter over the basil. Finish with lots of pepper.

Coronation Chicken Salad

This salad is a must-cook, you could leave out the cauliflower if you're short on time.

1 small cauliflower, cut into small florets, with its leaves
1 teaspoon ground cumin
1 tablespoon extra virgin olive oil
½ red onion, finely sliced
juice of 1 lemon
2 boneless skin-on chicken thighs, about 100g (3½oz) each
250g (9oz) cooked grains, from a pouch
50g (1¾oz) dried apricots, finely chopped
15g (½oz) coriander (cilantro) leaves
2 tablespoons flaked (sliced) almonds, toasted
salt and pepper

FOR THE DRESSING

220g (8oz) Greek-style yogurt
2½ teaspoons curry powder
3 teaspoons mango chutney
juice of ½ lemon

1 Preheat the air fryer to 180°C (350°F) for 4 minutes.

2 In a medium-sized bowl, mix together the cauliflower florets and their leaves with the cumin, olive oil and a pinch of salt. Place in the air fryer and cook for around 15 minutes until the cauliflower is tender and slightly charred, and the leaves have turned crispy. Transfer the cooked cauliflower to a medium-sized bowl and set aside.

3 Meanwhile, in a small bowl, mix the red onion with the lemon juice and a pinch of salt.

4 Place the chicken thighs into the air fryer, skin-side up. Season the skin with a little salt and cook for 15 minutes.

5 Meanwhile, in a bowl, whisk together all the dressing ingredients, along with a pinch of salt. Microwave the pouch of grains for 1 minute, then tip the grains into the bowl of cauliflower, along with the dried apricots, pickled red onion and coriander.

6 Slice the chicken into 2cm (¾ inch) strips, then place in the bowl of dressing and mix to coat.

7 Spread the grains and cauliflower mixture on a platter, top with the chicken and flaked almonds, then drizzle over any remaining dressing.

Squash with Blue Cheese Dressing

So simple to make. The bitter radicchio works really well against the sweet butternut squash, but if you can't get hold of it, chicory or Little Gem lettuce would also work nicely.

½ butternut squash, around 400g (14oz), peeled and cut into 2cm (¾ inch pieces)
1 tablespoon extra virgin olive oil
1 radicchio, leaves separated
salt and pepper

FOR THE DRESSING

60g (2¼oz) soured cream
70g (2½oz) blue cheese
3 tablespoons Greek yogurt
1 teaspoon white wine vinegar

1 Preheat the air fryer to 180°C (350°F) for 4 minutes.

2 Put the butternut squash into a medium-sized bowl, drizzle over the olive oil and season well with salt and pepper. Put it into the air fryer and cook for around 20 minutes until tender and starting to char.

3 Meanwhile, place all the dressing ingredients into a small blender and blitz until smooth.

4 Serve by mixing together the radicchio and butternut squash, then tossing with the dressing.

Fennel Clementine Salad

This salad has everything going on: it's bitter, sweet, crunchy and creamy. It would make an impressive side dish to a simple roast chicken, or even a perfect addition to the table on Christmas day.

1 large fennel bulb, finely sliced

1 large courgette (zucchini), sliced into ½cm (¼ inch) rounds

1 tablespoon extra virgin olive oil

2 clementines

1 burrata

½ radicchio, leaves separated

10g (¼oz) dill fronds

salt and pepper

FOR THE DRESSING

juice of 1 lemon

3 tablespoons extra virgin olive oil

1 Preheat the air fryer to 180°C (350°F) for 4 minutes.

2 Either place the fennel and courgette into a baking dish that fits in the air fryer, or use the section underneath the basket if your air fryer has one. Add the oil, a pinch of salt and a grind of pepper. Cook for 20 minutes until softened and charring in places.

3 Meanwhile, in a small bowl, whisk together the dressing ingredients until emulsified.

4 With a small knife, remove the clementine peel and cut the flesh into rounds or segments.

5 Plate up the fennel and courgette and place on the clementine. Tear the burrata into pieces and place over the salad. Follow with the radicchio, drizzle over the dressing and scatter over the dill, then grind over some pepper.

Soy Broccoli & Green Bean Salad

It doesn't get much simpler than this. Ten minutes in the air fryer and you have an unexpectedly flavourful salad that would work well as a side to your favourite protein.

200g (7oz) Tenderstem broccoli (broccolini)

100g (3½oz) green beans, ends trimmed

1 tablespoon extra virgin olive oil

2 tablespoons unsalted peanuts

2 teaspoons white or black sesame seeds

FOR THE DRESSING

1½ tablespoons soy sauce

1 tablespoon brown rice vinegar

1 teaspoon sesame oil

1 teaspoon mirin

1cm (½ inch) piece of root ginger, finely grated

1 Preheat the air fryer to 180°C (350°F) for 4 minutes.

2 Place the broccoli and green beans into the air fryer. Drizzle over the oil and cook for around 10 minutes until the beans are tender and the broccoli is charred in places.

3 Meanwhile, in a small bowl, mix together the dressing ingredients.

4 Put the beans and broccoli into a serving bowl, spoon over the dressing, sprinkle with the peanuts and sesame seeds, and serve.

Hispi Cabbage with Miso Butter

The air fryer achieves the perfect char on this cabbage, while the miso butter gives it a wonderful umami flavour. A star side dish!

1 hispi (sweetheart) cabbage, quartered lengthways through the core
2 tablespoons extra virgin olive oil
1 banana shallot, finely sliced into rings
juice of ½ lime
1 tablespoon white miso paste
30g (1oz) butter, softened
2 garlic cloves, bashed but kept in their skins
2 tablespoons crispy chilli oil
salt

FOR THE DRESSING
100g (3½oz) strained Greek yogurt
2 tablespoons extra virgin olive oil

1 Preheat the air fryer to 200°C (400°F) for 4 minutes.

2 Either put the cabbage wedges into a baking dish that fits in the air fryer, or use the section underneath the basket if your air fryer has one. Drizzle over the olive oil and cook for 10 minutes, until the edges are starting to char.

3 Meanwhile, in a small bowl, mix the shallot rings with the lime juice. Add a pinch of salt.

4 In another bowl, mix the miso into the softened butter and dot this over the cabbage wedges. Add the garlic and a splash of water.

5 Reduce the air fryer temperature to 180°C (350°F) and cook for 6 minutes, then remove the garlic and cook the cabbage for another 5 minutes until it is soft: you should be able to pierce through the core with a sharp knife.

6 Meanwhile, remove the skin from the garlic cloves and add them to a small blender, along with the dressing ingredients and a pinch of salt. Blitz to combine.

7 Serve the cabbage with the dressing, crispy chilli oil and lime-pickled shallot.

QUICK DINNERS

Prawn Tacos

FOR THE PICKLED CABBAGE

¼ red cabbage, finely shredded
½ red onion, finely chopped
juice of 1 lime
salt

FOR THE CHIPOTLE MAYO

1½ teaspoons chipotle paste
70g (2½oz) mayonnaise

FOR THE CORIANDER YOGURT

20g (¾oz) coriander (cilantro)
3 tablespoons strained Greek yogurt
juice of ½ lemon
½ garlic clove, roughly chopped

FOR THE PRAWNS

30g (1oz) plain (all-purpose) flour
2 eggs
50g (1¾oz) panko crumbs
1 teaspoon fajita seasoning
180g (6oz) raw king prawns (jumbo shrimp)
olive oil, or vegetable oil, for spraying
6 small tortilla wraps, or 4 large wraps

You can swap out the taco accompaniments as you please, but it's worth trying to make them all, as the combination is delicious.

1 Put the red cabbage into a medium-sized bowl with the red onion and lime juice. Sprinkle over a pinch of salt and mix, then set aside. In a small bowl, mix together the chipotle paste and mayo. Put all the ingredients for the coriander yogurt into a small blender with a pinch of salt and blitz until smooth.

2 Put the flour, eggs and panko into 3 separate small, shallow dishes. Season the flour with the fajita seasoning and a pinch of salt, and lightly beat the eggs with a fork.

3 Put a prawn into the flour, shake off the excess, then place into the egg, then into the panko. Repeat with all the prawns, putting the coated ones on a tray as you go.

4 Preheat the air fryer to 190°C (375°F) for 4 minutes.

5 Place the prawns into the air fryer basket, spray liberally with oil and cook for 2 minutes. Turn over and cook for another 2 minutes until golden.

6 Meanwhile, heat a frying pan over a medium heat. Once hot, heat the tortilla wraps for around 15 seconds on each side.

7 Spread the coriander yogurt on the wraps, then add the prawns, chipotle mayo and pickled red cabbage. Wrap and eat.

Chicken Burgers

Get crispy, juicy chicken without the guilt of a deep-fat fryer. If you want a quick fast food-style sauce, mix the mayo with the same quantities of ketchup and mustard and stir through some finely chopped pickles.

2 chicken breasts, total weight about 200g (7oz)
150g (5½ oz) buttermilk
½ teaspoon smoked paprika
¼ teaspoon cayenne pepper
½ teaspoon garlic powder
150g (5½ oz) cornflakes
olive oil, or vegetable oil, for spraying
salt and pepper

TO SERVE

2 burger buns
3 tablespoons mayonnaise
a few dill pickles, sliced
1 Little Gem lettuce

1 Place the chicken breasts in between 2 pieces of baking parchment (parchment paper) and bash with a rolling pin until 3cm (1 inch) thick. Put the chicken into a ziplock bag, then add the buttermilk, paprika, cayenne, garlic powder and a large pinch of salt. Squish together with your hands and leave to marinate in the fridge for at least 1 hour and up to 24 hours.

2 When ready to cook, preheat the air fryer to 190°C (375°F) for 4 minutes.

3 Put the cornflakes into a large ziplock bag and bash with a rolling pin until they resemble fine breadcrumbs. Grind in lots of pepper: around 20 twists. Take the chicken out of the marinade and dredge it in the cornflake crumbs, making sure every nook and cranny is coated.

4 Put the chicken into the air fryer, spray with oil and cook for 6 minutes. Then turn the chicken over, spray with more oil and cook for another 6 minutes until golden and crisp in places.

5 Meanwhile, toast the buns in a hot dry frying pan for 30 seconds, then spread the mayonnaise over the bottom bun. Pile on the pickles, lettuce and chicken, then add the bun lid and serve.

Baked Sweet Potatoes with Coriander Pesto

Creamy cannellini beans are livened up by this spicy coriander pesto. Baking potatoes in the air fryer couldn't be easier.

4 sweet potatoes

1 tablespoon extra virgin olive oil

400g (14oz) can cannellini (white) beans, rinsed and drained

salt and pepper

FOR THE PESTO

30g (1oz) coriander (cilantro), with stalks

1 green chilli (chile), deseeded and roughly chopped

½ garlic clove, roughly chopped

1 teaspoon ground cumin

20ml (4 teaspoons) extra virgin olive oil

juice of 1 lime

1 Preheat the air fryer to 180°C (350°F) for 4 minutes.

2 Prick the sweet potatoes all over with a fork. Rub the oil over their skins and season with salt and pepper. Place into the air fryer and cook for 20 minutes until soft. This may take a little longer, depending on the size of your potatoes.

3 Meanwhile, place all the pesto ingredients into a blender and pulse until smooth, but still retaining some texture. Season and set aside.

4 Cut the sweet potatoes open lengthways, spoon in the beans and return to the air fryer to cook for 2 minutes more, just to warm the beans.

5 Serve drizzled with the pesto.

Tofu with Tahini & Crispy Chilli

Call this your new midweek staple: with creamy tahini and fiery chilli oil, it is so satisfying to eat and easy to make.

280g (9¾oz) firm tofu, patted dry, cut into 2cm (¾ inch) cubes

2 tablespoons ketjap manis

1 teaspoon sesame oil

1 teaspoon garlic granules

200g (7oz) green beans, trimmed

olive oil, or vegetable oil, for spraying

1 tablespoon cornflour (corn starch)

250g (9oz) pouch of microwave rice

2 tablespoons crispy chilli oil

2 tablespoons roughly chopped coriander (cilantro)

salt

FOR THE TAHINI DRESSING

2 tablespoons tahini

2 tablespoons soy sauce

2 teaspoons maple syrup

juice of 1 lemon

1 Preheat the air fryer to 180°C (350°F) for 4 minutes.

2 Place the tofu in a medium-sized bowl and add the ketjap manis, sesame oil and garlic granules. Mix together.

3 Put the green beans into the section underneath the basket of the air fryer, if your air fryer has one. Spray with oil and season with a little salt. Add the cornflour to the tofu, mix well and put into the air fryer basket. Cook the beans and tofu for 20 minutes.

4 Meanwhile, in a small bowl, mix together all the dressing ingredients with a splash of water. Microwave the rice for 2½ minutes.

5 Divide the rice between 2 plates, top with the tofu and arrange the green beans on the side. Drizzle over the tahini dressing and crispy chilli oil, then sprinkle over the coriander and serve.

Roasted Tomato Pasta

Using good-quality tomatoes goes a long way here. If you can't get hold of Datterini tomatoes, you can make this dish with cherry tomatoes instead.

500g (1lb 2oz) Datterini tomatoes (or see recipe introduction)

4 garlic cloves, bashed but kept in their skins

¼ teaspoon chilli (red pepper) flakes

2 tablespoons extra virgin olive oil

200g (7oz) spaghetti

finely grated zest of 1 lemon

1 teaspoon Parmesan cheese (vegetarian if needed), finely grated

salt and pepper

a few basil leaves (optional)

1 Preheat the air fryer to 150°C (300°F) for 4 minutes.

2 Put the tomatoes, garlic and chilli flakes into a baking dish that fits in the air fryer, or you can use the section underneath the basket if your air fryer has one. Season well, add the oil and cook for 20–25 minutes.

3 Meanwhile, boil a large pot of water and season generously with salt. Once the water is boiling, add the pasta and cook according to the packet instructions. Once the pasta is almost cooked, reserve 1 cup of water, then drain the pasta in a sieve.

4 Squeeze the garlic cloves out of their skins and add to the tomatoes. Stir the tomatoes into the pasta with the lemon zest and some of the reserved pasta water, and keep mixing until you have a thick sauce.

5 Sprinkle over the Parmesan and basil leaves and grind over some pepper to serve.

Cod Goujons

A real crowd-pleaser, these goujons come out perfectly crisp, just like they would from a deep-fat fryer. Sprinkle them with salt as soon as they're done to make sure the seasoning hits.

3 tablespoons plain (all-purpose) flour
3 eggs
150g (5½oz) panko crumbs
1 teaspoon smoked paprika
300g (10½oz) cod fillets, skin removed, cut into 3cm (1 inch) strips
olive oil, or vegetable oil, for spraying
salt

FOR THE TARTARE SAUCE

4 tablespoons mayonnaise
2 teaspoons capers, roughly chopped
5g (⅛oz) flat-leaf parsley leaves, roughly chopped
finely grated zest of ½ lemon

1 Put the flour, eggs and panko into 3 separate small, shallow dishes. Season the flour with a pinch of salt and the panko with the paprika, then lightly beat the eggs with a fork.

2 Each goujon will have a double panko coating. Put a piece of cod into the flour, shake off the excess, then place into the egg, then into the panko. Repeat the egg and panko stage and set aside on a tray, then repeat with the remaining pieces of cod.

3 Preheat the air fryer to 190°C (375°F) for 4 minutes. Place the goujons into the air fryer, spray liberally with oil and cook for 6 minutes until cooked through and golden in colour.

4 Meanwhile, in a small bowl, mix together all the tartare sauce ingredients with a pinch of salt. Serve with the goujons.

Sausage & Fennel Traybake

The perfect traybake. Let the air fryer do all the work while you put your feet up.

1 large fennel bulb, thinly sliced
2 banana shallots, halved lengthways
2 rosemary sprigs
200g (7oz) baby new potatoes, larger ones quartered, smaller ones halved
1 tablespoon extra virgin olive oil
4 sausages
1 tablespoon sherry vinegar
20g (¾oz) feta cheese
15g (½oz) dill, leaves picked
pepper

TO SERVE

1 lemon, cut in wedges
Dijon mustard

1 Preheat the air fryer to 180°C (350°F) for 4 minutes.

2 In a baking dish that fits in the air fryer, or in the section underneath the basket if your air fryer has one, combine the fennel, shallots, rosemary and potatoes. Drizzle over the oil and add the sausages. Cook for 15 minutes.

3 Turn the sausages over and add the sherry vinegar and a splash of water. Cook for another 5–10 minutes until the sausages are brown and all the vegetables are tender.

4 Take the baking dish out of the air fryer. If you have used the section underneath the basket of the air fryer, transfer the ingredients to a baking dish.

5 Crumble over the feta, sprinkle with the dill and grind over some pepper. Serve with lemon wedges and a pot of Dijon mustard, if you wish.

Lamb Kofta Wraps

These heavenly spiced koftas are so delicious and couldn't be easier. If you have any left over, try serving them over some couscous. They freeze really well, too.

400g (14oz) minced (ground) lamb
1 teaspoon sumac, plus extra to finish
1 teaspoon za'atar
1 teaspoon ground coriander
½ teaspoon cayenne pepper
1 tablespoon ground cumin
finely grated zest of 1 lemon
2 tablespoons roughly chopped flat-leaf parsley leaves
4 flatbreads
150g (5½oz) hummus
2 Little Gem lettuces
4 tablespoons pomegranate seeds
salt and pepper
extra virgin olive oil, to serve

1 Preheat the air fryer to 170°C (340°F) for 4 minutes.

2 In a medium-sized bowl, mix together the lamb and all the dried herbs and spices, then season well with salt. Add the lemon zest and parsley. Form into small kofta shapes, around 50g (1¾oz) each. Place into the air fryer and cook for 6 minutes until cooked through.

3 Meanwhile, heat a frying pan over a medium heat. Once hot, heat the flatbreads for around 15 seconds on each side.

4 To serve, spread the hummus over the flatbreads, then top with the lettuce and koftas, sprinkle over the pomegranate seeds. Finish with a drizzle of oil and a grind of pepper.

Cheesy Artichoke Tarts

These are rich and delicious, and make for an impressive light dinner for guests if you serve them with a simple dressed salad.

1 sheet of ready-rolled puff pastry

30g (1oz) Gruyère cheese (vegetarian if needed), grated

30g (1oz) Cheddar cheese, grated

4 tablespoons double (heavy) cream

2 jarred artichokes, around 50g (1¾oz), quartered

1 egg, lightly beaten

pepper

1 Unroll the pastry sheet and cut into 4 squares, each about 10 x 10cm (4 inches). Save any leftover pastry for another use.

2 With a small, sharp knife, score a 2cm (¾ inch) border around each pastry square. Place on a tray and put into the fridge.

3 In a small bowl, combine both cheeses with the cream and a pinch of pepper.

4 Take the pastry squares out of the fridge. Dot the cheese mixture in the middle of the squares, avoiding the borders. Top with the artichokes and brush the borders with the egg.

5 Preheat the air fryer to 180°C (350°F) for 4 minutes. Place the tarts into the air fryer and cook for 11 minutes, until risen and golden.

Butternut Squash Mac & Cheese

The key to an epic macaroni cheese is combining different cheeses; here, I've used Cheddar and Parmesan, and a dash of crème fraîche for extra tang. The butternut squash elevates the flavour, resulting in the ultimate comfort dinner.

½ butternut squash, about 500g (1lb 2oz), peeled and cut into 2cm (¾ inch) cubes
1 tablespoon extra virgin olive oil
1½ teaspoons caraway seeds
½ teaspoon cayenne pepper
200g (7oz) macaroni
3 tablespoons crème fraîche
100g (3½oz) Cheddar cheese, grated
30g (1oz) Parmesan cheese (vegetarian, if needed), finely grated
2 tablespoons pumpkin seeds, toasted
salt and pepper

1 Preheat the air fryer to 180°C (350°F) for 4 minutes. In a medium-sized bowl, mix together the butternut squash, olive oil, caraway and cayenne. Put into the air fryer and cook for 20 minutes until soft.

2 Meanwhile, fill a large saucepan with water and heavily season with salt. Bring to the boil and cook the macaroni for 2 minutes less than the packet instructs. Reserve half a cup of the pasta water. Drain the macaroni into a sieve and run under cold water to stop the cooking.

3 Place three-quarters of the butternut squash into a blender with the crème fraîche. Add some of the reserved pasta water, season with salt and blitz until smooth. If it still looks very thick, then add some more water; you want it to look saucy.

4 Put the macaroni into a large bowl with three-quarters of both cheeses and add both the blitzed and reserved cubes of butternut squash. Season with salt and pepper.

5 Reduce the temperature of the air fryer to 170°C (340°F). Put the macaroni into a dish that fits into the air fryer, about 19cm (7½ inches), sprinkle over the remaining cheese and cook for around 10 minutes until the cheese has melted and the top is turning slightly crispy.

6 Sprinkle over the pumpkin seeds and serve.

Pea & Mint Falafel Pittas

These are cheap, easy and fun to make, and the freshness of mint really brings them to life. You could easily double the batch and freeze (before frying them) to cook another day.

FOR THE FALAFEL

400g (14oz) can chickpeas, drained and rinsed

200g (7oz) frozen peas, defrosted

½ garlic clove, roughly chopped

15g (½oz) mint leaves, roughly chopped

1 teaspoon ground cumin

finely grated zest of 1 lemon

60g (2¼oz) plain (all-purpose) flour

olive oil, or vegetable oil, for spraying

salt

FOR THE PITTAS

3 pitta breads

3 tablespoons hummus

1 Little Gem lettuce, leaves separated

2 large tomatoes, sliced

½ cucumber, sliced

1 Tip the chickpeas and peas on to a tray and pat dry with kitchen paper (paper towels). Place into a blender and add the garlic, mint, cumin and lemon zest, then season generously with salt. Pulse-blend, but don't overmix; you want a coarse mixture. Add the flour and pulse a few more times until combined.

2 Shape the mixture into 9 balls. Put these on a tray and place in the fridge for 15 minutes, or in the freezer for 5 minutes. Preheat the air fryer to 200°C (400°F) for 4 minutes.

3 Put the falafels into the air fryer. Spray liberally with oil and cook for 20 minutes.

4 Meanwhile, toast the pittas.

5 Fill the pittas with hummus, lettuce leaves, tomatoes, cucumber and falafel.

Halloumi with Romesco & Pitta Chips

The air fryer ensures this halloumi comes out perfectly golden, with minimal effort, every time. This smoky romesco is the ideal summer sauce and would also work well with a steak. A splendid quick dinner!

2 pitta breads, cut into small triangles
olive oil, or vegetable oil, for spraying
1 teaspoon za'atar
225g (8oz) halloumi cheese, cut into 2cm (¾ inch) slices
salt and pepper

FOR THE ROMESCO SAUCE

½ jar (225g/8oz) roasted red peppers (bell peppers)
60g (2¼oz) blanched (skinned) almonds
1 tablespoon sherry vinegar
½ garlic clove, roughly chopped
½ teaspoon sweet paprika
40ml (1½fl oz) extra virgin olive oil

1 Preheat the air fryer to 180°C (350°F) for 4 minutes.

2 Put the pitta triangles into the air fryer, spray with a little oil and cook for 5 minutes. Turn the pitta chips over and cook for another 3 minutes. Sprinkle with the za'atar and some salt, then set aside.

3 Meanwhile, place all the ingredients for the romesco sauce in a food processor, along with a generous pinch of salt and pepper. Blitz to combine, then set aside.

4 Increase the air fryer temperature to 190°C (375°F). Add the halloumi to the air fryer, spray with a little oil and cook for 5 minutes. Turn over and cook for another 5 minutes until golden.

5 Serve the halloumi with the romesco sauce and pitta chips.

SERVES 2 · 35 MINS · VE VEGAN

Miso Aubergine

Sweet, sharp and umami, this is the kind of sauce that has you licking the plate clean. A fuss-free vegan classic.

2 aubergines (eggplants)
olive oil, or vegetable oil, for spraying
1 tablespoon red or white miso paste
1 tablespoon soy sauce
1 teaspoon brown rice vinegar
1 teaspoon maple syrup
250g (9oz) pouch of microwave rice
1 spring onion (scallion), finely sliced
1 red chilli (chile), finely sliced
1 teaspoon black sesame seeds

1 Preheat the air fryer to 170°C (340°F) for 4 minutes.

2 Cut the aubergines in half lengthways and score a criss-cross pattern into the flesh. Put into the air fryer flesh-side up, spray liberally with oil and cook for 20 minutes.

3 In a small bowl, whisk together the miso, soy sauce, rice vinegar and maple syrup. Add 1 tablespoon of hot water and mix again until smooth. Brush the mix over the aubergines and cook for another 10 minutes.

4 Meanwhile, microwave the rice for 2½ minutes.

5 Serve the aubergine alongside the rice, sprinkling over the spring onion, chilli and sesame seeds.

Tonnato Steak

Tonnato is a tuna- and anchovy-based Italian dressing. It's so easy to make and packs a real punch. As an alternative, just serve the steak with some air fryer chips and a simple salad.

1 × 3cm (1 inch) thick sirloin (porterhouse) steak, about 400g (14oz)
1 tablespoon extra virgin olive oil
40g rocket (arugula)
200g (7oz) cherry tomatoes, halved
2 tablespoons crispy shallots
salt and pepper

FOR THE DRESSING

150g (5½oz) can tuna, drained (112g/4oz drained weight)
3 anchovy fillets
½ garlic clove
2 egg yolks
85ml (3fl oz) extra virgin olive oil
1 tablespoon white wine vinegar
juice of ½ lemon
1 tablespoon capers

1 Take the steak out of the fridge at least 30 minutes before cooking. Preheat the air fryer to 200°C (400°F) for 4 minutes.

2 Rub both sides of the steak with the olive oil, then add a generous sprinkle of salt and pepper to both sides. Put the steak into the air fryer and cook for 8 minutes, turning over halfway through. Once ready, rest the steak for 5–10 minutes. This timing should give you the perfect medium-rare steak.

3 Meanwhile, prepare the dressing. Put the tuna, anchovy, garlic and egg yolks into a blender. Blitz, gradually drizzling in the olive oil, until emulsified. Stir in the vinegar, lemon juice and capers. The sauce should be thick, but you should still be able to easily drizzle it. If it is looking too thick, just add a splash of water.

4 To serve, scatter the rocket on a platter, then top with the sliced steak, tomatoes, dressing and crispy shallots.

WEEKEND EATS

Beetroot Side of Salmon

Earthy beetroot with salmon is such a fantastic combination. This makes an impressive meal for a special occasion.

250g (9oz) raw beetroot (beets), cut into 4cm (1½ inch) cubes
3 garlic cloves, bashed but kept in their skins
2 tablespoons extra virgin olive oil
200g (7oz) Tenderstem broccoli (broccolini)
side of salmon, about 500g (1lb 2oz)
2 tablespoons strained Greek yogurt
1 tablespoon sherry vinegar
½ teaspoon sumac
salt and black pepper
rye bread, to serve (optional)

1 Preheat the air fryer to 170°C (340°F) for 4 minutes.

2 Put the beetroot and garlic on to a piece of foil in the air fryer basket, then drizzle over 1 tablespoon of the oil and cook for 20 minutes. Remove the garlic, increase the temperature to 180°C (350°F) and cook the beetroot for a further 10 minutes until tender. Remove and set aside. Reduce the air fryer temperature to 170°C (340°F).

3 Place the broccoli in the section underneath the air fryer basket if you have one (otherwise place in the basket), and drizzle with the remaining 1 tablespoon of oil.

4 Put the salmon on a piece of foil or baking parchment (parchment paper) and place this in the air fryer basket. Cook for 10 minutes until the flesh of the salmon is firm and coral pink in colour, and the broccoli is tender.

5 Meanwhile, squeeze the garlic cloves out of their skins and add to a blender along with the beetroot, Greek yogurt, sherry vinegar and some salt. Blitz and set aside.

6 Serve the salmon with the broccoli and the beetroot sauce and sprinkle over the sumac and a grind of black pepper. Offer rye bread on the side, if you like.

Duck Pancakes

You'll be so impressed with yourself when you've tasted these! You'll never need to order them from a takeaway again.

2 duck breasts, around 150g (5½oz) each
1 tablespoon honey
1 teaspoon five spice
1 pack of Chinese-style pancakes
½ cucumber, cut into matchsticks
1 bunch of spring onions (scallions), finely shredded
plum sauce (optional)
salt

1　If you have time, salt the skin of the duck and place it in the fridge overnight. Remove the duck from the fridge at least 30 minutes before you are ready to cook.

2　Preheat the air fryer to 150°C (300°F) for 4 minutes.

3　In a small bowl, mix together the honey and five spice. Brush this over the duck, put into the air fryer basket and cook for 12 minutes, then increase the heat to 180°C (350°F) for a further 4 minutes until the duck is cooked through. Leave to rest for 10 minutes.

4　Microwave the pancakes for 1 minute.

5　Finely shred the duck and serve it with the pancakes, cucumber, spring onions and plum sauce.

 SERVES 2　🕐 10 MINS　 VEGAN

Crispy 'Seaweed'

A perfect addition to a larger feast. This would go well with my Duck pancakes (above) or Prawn toasts (see page 47).

200g (7oz) kale, stalks removed, finely shredded
1 teaspoon five spice
½ teaspoon dark brown soft sugar
2 tablespoons vegetable oil

1　Preheat the air fryer to 200°C (400°F) for 4 minutes.

2　Put the kale into a medium-sized bowl and add the five spice, sugar and oil, then mix.

3　Transfer to the air fryer and cook for 5 minutes until crispy.

SERVES 2   **35 MINS**   VG **VEGETARIAN OPTION**

Courgette Galette

You'll love this shatteringly crisp puff pastry with a combination of creamy mascarpone and courgette. Ricotta would also work really well here.

1 large courgette (zucchini), sliced into ½ cm (¼ inch) rounds
¼ teaspoon chilli (red pepper) flakes
1 tablespoon extra virgin olive oil
2 tablespoons mascarpone
20g (¾oz) Parmesan cheese (vegetarian, if needed), finely grated
finely grated zest of 1 lemon
1 × 320g (11½oz) sheet of ready-rolled shortcrust pastry
1 egg, lightly beaten
salt and pepper

1 Put the courgette into a medium-sized bowl with the chilli flakes and oil. Season with salt and pepper, mix and set aside.

2 In a small bowl, mix together the mascarpone, 15g (½oz) of the Parmesan and the lemon zest.

3 Unroll the pastry and cut out a 20cm (8 inch) circle. Spread out the mascarpone mixture in the middle, leaving a 3cm (1 inch) border around the edges. Top with the courgettes, overlapping the slices until you have used them all. Fold in the edges of the pastry and brush these pastry edges with egg. Preheat the air fryer to 190°C (375°F) for 4 minutes.

4 Put the galette into the air fryer basket and cook for 25 minutes, until the pastry is golden and the courgettes are soft. Sprinkle over the remaining Parmesan and serve.

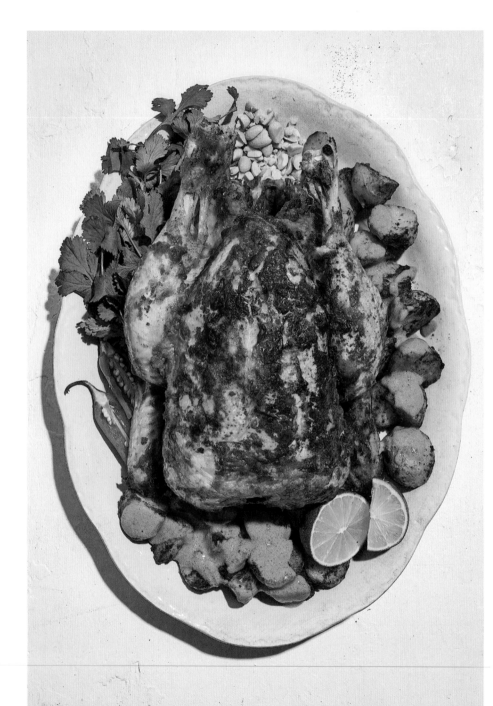

Whole Chicken Satay

An air fryer is great for roasting a whole chicken without dealing with lots of trays and pans. This satay sauce is so moreish; try serving it with some quick-pickled cucumber for extra freshness.

1 medium whole chicken, around 1.6kg (3lb 8oz)

200g (7oz) baby new potatoes, larger ones quartered, smaller ones halved

FOR THE SATAY SAUCE

4 tablespoons red curry paste

150g (5½oz) peanut butter

2 tablespoons soy sauce

juice of 1 lime

400ml (14oz) can coconut milk

1 teaspoon caster sugar

2cm (¾ inch) piece of root ginger, roughly chopped

2 garlic cloves, roughly chopped

TO SERVE

2 tablespoons unsalted roasted peanuts, roughly chopped

1 red chilli (chile), finely sliced

25g (1oz) coriander (cilantro), leaves picked

2 limes, cut into wedges

1 Put all the satay sauce ingredients into a blender and blitz until smooth. Put the chicken into a large ziplock bag and pour in half the satay sauce. Leave to marinate in the fridge for at least 1 hour and up to 24 hours. Set the remaining satay sauce aside. Take the chicken out of the fridge at least 30 minutes before you are ready to cook.

2 Preheat the air fryer to 160°C (325°F) for 4 minutes.

3 Remove the chicken from the bag and scrape off most of the marinade, reserving it for later. Put the chicken into the air fryer, breast-side down. Cook for 40 minutes. Turn over the chicken and brush on some of the reserved marinade. Increase the temperature of the air fryer to 170°C (340°F) and cook for a further 10–15 minutes until cooked through. Remove the chicken from the air fryer and leave to rest.

4 Put the potatoes into the chicken juices and satay sauce left behind in the air fryer and toss to coat. Increase the temperature to 190°C (375°F) and cook for around 20 minutes until tender and taking on colour.

5 Meanwhile, in a saucepan, heat the remaining satay sauce over a low-medium heat until slightly thickened.

6 Arrange the chicken on a platter with the potatoes and scatter with the peanuts, chilli and coriander. Serve with lime wedges and the satay sauce.

Sea Bass with Soy & Ginger

The air fryer gives the sea bass a beautifully crisp, golden exterior. This is a simple way to impress. Serve with rice or noodles for a more substantial feast.

1–2 whole sea bass, gutted and cleaned, total weight around 500g (1lb 2oz)

3 tablespoons soy sauce

1 teaspoon caster (superfine) sugar

4 tablespoons vegetable oil

3cm (1 inch) piece of root ginger, cut into matchsticks

3 garlic cloves, cut into matchsticks

25g (1oz) coriander (cilantro) leaves

1 spring onion (scallion), finely sliced

1 red chilli (chile), finely sliced

1 lime, cut into wedges

rice or noodles, to serve (optional)

1 Preheat the air fryer to 200°C (400°F) for 4 minutes.

2 With a sharp knife, score 3 diagonal slashes on either side of the fish.

3 Put the soy sauce on a plate or baking tray and roll both sides of the fish in the soy. Sprinkle the sugar over both sides of the fish, then place into the air fryer basket. Cook for 6 minutes. Remove the fish from the air fryer and place on a platter.

4 Heat the oil in a small saucepan over a high heat. Once the oil is very hot, add the ginger and garlic and fry for around 30 seconds, then pour this over the fish.

5 Arrange the coriander around the fish and sprinkle over the spring onion and chilli. Serve with lime wedges and rice or noodles, if you like.

Spinach & Ricotta Lasagne

Using fresh lasagne sheets here is an amazing air fryer hack for pasta dishes. Spinach and ricotta make a winning combination; you can't go wrong.

260g (9½oz) spinach, washed, stalks removed
25g (1oz) butter
25g (1oz) plain (all-purpose) flour
400ml (14fl oz) whole milk
100g (3½oz) ricotta
finely grated zest of 1 lemon
4–5 fresh lasagne sheets, total weight around 250g (9oz)
3 tablespoons pesto (vegetarian, if needed)
40g (1½oz) Parmesan cheese (vegetarian, if needed), finely grated
salt and pepper

1 Boil a kettle and place the spinach into a colander. Pour some of the boiled water over the spinach to wilt, then leave to cool.

2 Melt the butter in a saucepan over a low-medium heat, then add the flour and whisk for 1 minute. Gradually add the milk, whisking constantly so that there are no lumps, and cook until you have a thick white bechamel. Season with salt and set aside.

3 Put the ricotta and lemon zest into a medium-sized bowl. Squeeze the spinach to remove excess water, then finely chop and mix into the ricotta along with a ladle of the bechamel. Season with salt and pepper.

4 Preheat the air fryer to 170°C (340°F) for 4 minutes.

5 In a square dish that fits into the air fryer, about 19cm (7½ inches), assemble the lasagne. Lay in a lasagne sheet; you may need to cut these down to fit inside the dish. Then spread over a large spoonful of bechamel, followed by the spinach mix. Dot over the pesto and finish by sprinkling over some Parmesan. Repeat until you have 4–5 layers, finishing with bechamel and Parmesan.

6 Place into the air fryer and cook for around 30 minutes, until the lasagne is golden and cooked through. If it starts to take on too much colour, place a lid on the dish if it has one. If not, cover with foil, but make sure to tuck the foil underneath the dish so that it holds it down. You do not want it to fly around, as it can be dangerous. Serve.

Romano Peppers with Picada

This makes an perfect impressive vegan meal. If you want to add cheese, try goat's cheese here. Don't panic if you can't find romano peppers; any sweet pepper works well.

4 romano peppers, halved lengthways and deseeded
2 tablespoons extra virgin olive oil
250g (9oz) pouch of cooked grains, red rice, quinoa or similar
1 tablespoon sherry vinegar
1 teaspoon sweet paprika
salt and pepper

FOR THE PICADA

50g (1¾oz) sourdough bread, cut into 3cm (1 inch) pieces
2 garlic cloves, finely sliced
1 tablespoon extra virgin olive oil
15g (½oz) blanched (skinned) almonds
finely grated zest of 1 lemon
5g (⅛oz) flat-leaf parsley
salt

1 Preheat the air fryer to 180°C (350°F) for 4 minutes. Put the pepper halves on a piece of foil, cut-sides up, then drizzle over 1 tablespoon of the olive oil and season with salt and pepper. Place into the air fryer and cook for 10 minutes until slightly softened.

2 Meanwhile, in a medium-sized bowl, mix together the grains, the remaining 1 tablespoon of oil, the sherry vinegar and paprika. Season with salt and black pepper. Spoon this mixture into the cooked pepper halves and set aside.

3 For the picada, put the bread on another piece of foil, along with the garlic. Drizzle over the oil and put into the air fryer. Cook for 5 minutes. Remove the garlic and cook the bread for another 3–4 minutes until golden and crisp.

4 Put the bread, garlic and remaining picada ingredients into a blender and pulse to a coarse mix. Divide the picada between the peppers.

5 Place the peppers back into the air fryer and cook, still at 180°C (350°F), for 5 minutes until the picada starts to turn slightly crispy and the peppers are soft.

Porcini Mushroom Shepherd's Pie

Porcini mushrooms are an incredible store-cupboard staple and give a deep and meaty flavour to plant-based dishes. You've probably got everything you need for this recipe in the fridge, or knocking around the kitchen.

30g (1oz) dried porcini mushrooms
1 small onion, finely chopped
1 celery stick, finely chopped
1 small carrot, finely chopped
1 tablespoon extra virgin olive oil
1 tablespoon tomato purée (paste)
1 teaspoon red or white miso paste
1½ teaspoons plain (all-purpose) flour
1 tablespoon soy sauce
250g (9oz) pouch of cooked Puy lentils
250g (9oz) ready-made mashed potatoes (vegan, if needed)
salt and pepper

1 Boil a kettle, put the mushrooms into a measuring jug and cover with 300ml (½ pint) of boiling water. Set aside for around 30 minutes.

2 Preheat the air fryer to 160°C (325°F) for 4 minutes.

3 Either put the onion, celery and carrot into a baking dish that fits in the air fryer (around 19cm/7½ inches), or use the section underneath the basket if your air fryer has one. Drizzle over the oil, add a pinch of salt, and cook for 10 minutes. Stir, then cook for 10–15 minutes more until softened.

4 Reserving the soaking liquid, drain the mushrooms, then finely chop. Add the mushrooms and their liquid to the vegetables, along with the tomato purée, miso paste, flour, soy sauce and lentils. Season with salt and pepper. Increase the temperature to 170°C (340°F), stir and cook for 10 minutes.

5 If the mushroom mix is in the section underneath the air fryer basket, transfer it to the baking dish.

6 Top with the mash and cook for 25–30 minutes until golden.

Orzo with Prawns & Salsa Verde

'Nduja and prawns make a delicious combination, while the salsa verde here creates a freshness that really lifts this dish to the next level.

160g (5¾oz) orzo
1 tablespoon 'nduja
1 tablespoon butter
160g (5¾oz) raw king prawns (jumbo shrimp)
salt and pepper

FOR THE SALSA VERDE

15g (½oz) flat-leaf parsley
10g (¼oz) basil leaves
5g (1/8oz) mint leaves
1 tablespoon capers
1 anchovy fillet
4 tablespoons extra virgin olive oil
1 tablespoon red wine vinegar
1 teaspoon caster (superfine) sugar

1 Bring a large pot of water to the boil and season generously with salt. Once the water is boiling, add the orzo and cook according to the packet instructions. Drain and transfer to a baking dish that fits into the air fryer, around 19cm (7½ inches).

2 Preheat the air fryer to 170°C (340°F) for 4 minutes.

3 Dot the 'nduja and butter over the orzo, then cook for 2 minutes. Season with salt and pepper, then stir.

4 Add the prawns and cook for a further 2 minutes until the prawns are cooked through and the orzo is turning slightly crisp on top.

5 Meanwhile, finely chop the parsley, basil, mint, capers and anchovy, then add to a small bowl, along with the oil, red wine vinegar and sugar. Season with salt and mix.

6 Serve the orzo with the salsa verde.

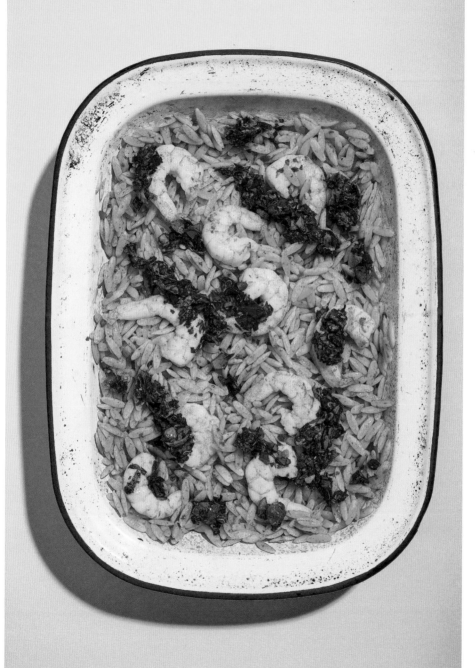

Pitta Pizzas

If you are short on time and in need of a quick dinner that can be ready in a matter of minutes, this one's for you. You can substitute the toppings for whatever you have in the fridge.

2 round pitta breads

4 tablespoons tomato passata

70g (2½oz) grated mozzarella cheese

½ red onion, finely sliced

2 tablespoons pitted black olives, halved

1 tablespoon extra virgin olive oil

1 Preheat the air fryer to 190°C (375°F) for 4 minutes.

2 Spread the passata over the pitta breads and scatter over the mozzarella. Top with the red onion and black olives.

3 Drizzle over the olive oil and cook for 6 minutes until the cheese has melted and the pizzas are crisp.

Pork Cutlets with Tahini

A herby tahini dressing works so well with pork. The pork medallion is an underrated cheap cut that really benefits from a punchy sauce. These cutlets would also be fantastic served with baked sweet potatoes.

350g (12oz) new potatoes, smaller ones left whole, larger ones halved
olive oil, or vegetable oil, for spraying
2 pork medallions, about 120g (4¼oz) each
2 tablespoons plain (all-purpose) flour
1 egg
70g (2½oz) panko crumbs
2 tablespoons sherry vinegar
salt

FOR THE TAHINI DRESSING

15g (½oz) coriander (cilantro)
15g (½oz) flat-leaf parsley
1 garlic clove, roughly chopped
2 tablespoons tahini
juice of ½ lemon
1 tablespoon extra virgin olive oil

1 Preheat the air fryer to 190°C (375°F) for 4 minutes. Put the potatoes into the section underneath the basket if your air fryer has one (or you can place in the main section). Spray them with oil, then season with salt and cook for 20 minutes.

2 Meanwhile, put the pork medallions between 2 sheets of baking parchment (parchment paper) and bash with a rolling pin until they are 2cm (¾ inch) thick.

3 Put the flour, egg and panko into 3 separate small, shallow dishes. Season the flour with a pinch of salt and lightly beat the egg with a fork. Place a pork medallion into the flour, shake off the excess, then place into the egg, then into the panko.

4 Line the air fryer with an air fryer liner or baking parchment (parchment paper) that has been pierced with holes and put the pork into the air fryer basket alongside the potatoes (if they are still cooking). Spray liberally with oil and cook for 6 minutes. Turn over, then spray with more oil and cook for a further 6 minutes until golden and cooked through.

5 Meanwhile, put the tahini dressing ingredients into a blender and blitz until smooth. If the dressing is looking too thick, add a little water.

6 Add the sherry vinegar to the potatoes and stir, then serve with the pork and tahini dressing.

Soy-Glazed Pork Belly

Great for entertaining, and so easy to prepare. You can marinate the pork up to 24 hours before cooking.

600g (1lb 5oz) pork belly slices

2 × 250g (9oz) pouches of microwave rice

FOR THE MARINADE

4 garlic cloves, finely grated

3cm (1 inch) piece of root ginger, finely grated

3 tablespoons soy sauce

1 tablespoon sesame oil

2 teaspoons brown rice vinegar

2 tablespoons ketjap manis

2 teaspoons honey

1 In a medium-sized bowl, mix together the marinade ingredients, along with 2 tablespoons of water. Add the pork belly slices and coat them in the marinade. Cover and leave to marinate for at least 1 hour.

2 Preheat the air fryer to 180°C (350°F) for 4 minutes.

3 Put the pork belly slices into the air fryer and cook for 10 minutes. Flip them over, then brush with the remaining marinade. Cook for another 10 minutes, until cooked through and charred in places.

4 Meanwhile, microwave the rice for 2½ minutes. Serve the pork with the rice.

SOMETHING SWEET

Baked Peaches
with Thyme

An incredibly simple, sweet and delicious dessert. If you reduce the sugar, you could also serve these with my Granola (see page 18) for breakfast.

2 large, ripe peaches, de-stoned and halved

2 tablespoons maple syrup

2 teaspoons demerara (turbinado) sugar

3 tablespoons natural yogurt

2 tablespoons flaked (sliced) almonds, toasted

2 thyme sprigs, leaves picked

1 Preheat the air fryer to 190°C (375°F) for 4 minutes.

2 Lay the peach halves, cut-sides up, on a sheet of foil. Drizzle over the maple syrup and sprinkle over the sugar.

3 Put into the air fryer and cook for 15 minutes, until the peaches have softened but are still holding their shape.

4 Serve with the yogurt, drizzling over the juices released during cooking and sprinkling with the almonds and thyme leaves.

Rhubarb Tartlets

Show-stopping tarts that are sharp and sweet and so easy to prepare. If you can't get hold of rhubarb, raspberries would also work well here.

1 × 320g (11½oz) sheet of ready-rolled puff pastry
4 rhubarb sticks, cut into 3cm (1 inch) batons
2 tablespoons light brown soft sugar
1 teaspoon ground cinnamon
4 tablespoons shop-bought custard (vanilla pudding)
1 tablespoon demerara (turbinado) sugar
1 egg, lightly beaten
icing sugar, to serve (optional)

1 Unroll the pastry sheet and cut into 4 squares, each about 10 × 10cm (4 inches). Save any leftover pastry for another use. With a small, sharp knife, score a 2cm (¾ inch) border around each pastry square, then place in the fridge on a tray.

2 Put the rhubarb batons into a medium-sized bowl with the brown sugar and cinnamon, then mix.

3 Preheat the air fryer to 170°C (340°F) for 4 minutes.

4 Spread 1 tablespoon of custard into the middle of each pastry square, avoiding the border, then arrange the rhubarb mixture on top of the custard.

5 Sprinkle the demerara sugar on top and brush the beaten egg over the borders.

6 Bake for 15 minutes, until the pastry is golden and the rhubarb is tender. Dust with icing sugar, if you like, and serve.

Churros

You know them, you love them and now you can make them in the air fryer! Try dipping these crunchy treats in white chocolate for some extra sweetness.

25g (1oz) butter
1 teaspoon caster (superfine) sugar
½ teaspoon vanilla extract
35g (1¼oz) plain (all-purpose) flour
1 small egg

TO FINISH

4 tablespoons granulated sugar
2 teaspoons ground cinnamon
50ml (1¾fl oz) shop-bought chocolate sauce

1 Put the butter, caster sugar, vanilla extract and 65ml (4 tablespoons) water into a saucepan, then bring to the boil. As soon as you see the water at the edges of the pan start to bubble, turn off the heat and quickly add the flour. Beat with a wooden spoon until the dough starts to come away from the sides of the pan and forms into a ball. Spread the mixture out on a plate to cool.

2 Once cool, transfer the mixture into a medium-sized bowl. Add the egg and beat vigorously until smooth and elastic. You can also do this in a stand mixer fitted with the paddle attachment. Transfer the mixture to a piping bag fitted with a star nozzle.

3 Preheat the air fryer to 190°C (375°F) for 4 minutes.

4 Line the air fryer with an air fryer liner or baking parchment (parchment paper) that has been pierced with holes, pipe in 6 churros and cook for 10–12 minutes until puffed up and golden.

5 Meanwhile, in a small, shallow bowl, mix together the granulated sugar and cinnamon.

6 Roll the churros in the cinnamon sugar, drizzle over the chocolate sauce and serve.

Blood Orange Olive Oil Cake

This olive oil cake is so moist and delicious. If you can't get hold of blood oranges, just use regular oranges instead.

130ml (4¾fl oz) extra virgin olive oil, plus more for the tin
200g (7oz) caster (superfine) sugar
finely grated zest of 2 blood oranges, plus the juice of 1
2 eggs
200g (7oz) plain (all-purpose) flour
1½ teaspoons baking powder
½ teaspoon fine salt
90ml (3¼fl oz) natural yogurt

1 Oil and line a 19cm (7½ inch) round baking tin with baking parchment (parchment paper). Preheat the air fryer to 150°C (300°F) for 4 minutes.

2 Put the sugar into a medium-sized bowl with the orange zest. Pour in the olive oil and whisk for 1 minute, using electric beaters. Add the eggs, one at a time, beating until combined.

3 Add the flour, baking powder, salt, yogurt and orange juice, then whisk until smooth.

4 Pour the mixture into the prepared tin and cook for 35–40 minutes. Insert a skewer: if it comes out clean, the cake is ready.

5 Turn off the air fryer but leave the cake in there for 10 minutes, then take it out and place on a wire rack to cool completely.

White Chocolate Pistachio Cookies

These are sweet and nutty. If your cookies puff up during the cooking process, simply press them down lightly with the back of a dessert spoon as soon as you take them out, for that crackly signature look.

85g (3oz) butter, softened
100g (3½oz) soft light brown sugar
1 egg
1 teaspoon vanilla extract
120g (4¼oz) plain (all-purpose) flour
1 teaspoon cornflour (corn starch)
¼ teaspoon fine salt
70g (2½oz) white chocolate, roughly chopped
50g (1¾oz) unsalted pistachios, roughly chopped
30g (1oz) dried apricots, roughly chopped

1 Put the butter and sugar into a medium-sized bowl. Using electric beaters or a stand mixer, whisk until the mix is pale and light. Add the egg and vanilla extract and mix until smooth.

2 Put the flour into a separate medium-sized bowl. Add the cornflour and salt, then mix. Add the dry mixture to the wet bit by bit, gradually mixing it in. Stir in the chocolate, pistachios and apricots. Cover and chill for 1–2 hours.

3 When ready to cook, preheat the air fryer to 170°C (340°F) for 4 minutes.

4 Roll the dough into balls of around 40g (1½oz) each. Line the air fryer with an air fryer liner or baking parchment (parchment paper) that has been pierced with holes, put in the rolled cookie balls and cook for 10–12 minutes until golden. Press down with the back of a spoon if they have puffed up. Leave to cool on a wire rack.

Miso Brown Butter Apple Crumble

The miso brown butter here gives this crumble a nutty, savoury flavour. Swap the apples for pears, plums, rhubarb or whatever fruit is in season.

FOR THE CRUMBLE

100g (3½oz) butter, cubed

1 tablespoon white miso paste

120g (4½oz) plain (all-purpose) flour

30g (1oz) rolled oats

65g (2½oz) light brown soft sugar

1 tablespoon demerara (turbinado) sugar

FOR THE FILLING

3 Bramley (cooker) apples, about 450g (1lb) total weight, peeled and cut into 3cm (1 inch) chunks

2 tablespoons soft brown sugar

1 teaspoon cornflour (corn starch)

2 teaspoons vanilla paste

1 To make the crumble, melt the butter in a medium-sized saucepan over a low-medium heat. Cook until the butter starts to foam and smell nutty. This should take 3–5 minutes. Take the pan off the heat and whisk in the miso paste, then set aside to cool slightly.

2 In a medium-sized bowl, mix together the flour, oats and soft brown sugar. Pour the miso butter over this and mix. Spread out on a tray and put into the freezer for 15 minutes.

3 To make the filling, tip the apple chunks into a medium-sized bowl with the sugar, cornflour and vanilla. Stir to combine, then tip into a round dish that fits into the air fryer, about 19cm (7½ inches).

4 Preheat the air fryer to 160°C (325°F) for 4 minutes.

5 Top the apple filling with the crumble mix, sprinkle over the demerara sugar and cook for 30 minutes until golden.

S'mores

Simple and delicious, a quick sweet treat that can be made in a matter of minutes. Play around with different types of biscuit, or swap the chocolate for chocolate and hazelnut spread.

4 Rich Tea biscuits, or graham crackers
4 milk chocolate squares
2 large marshmallows

1 Preheat the air fryer to 180°C (350°F) for 4 minutes.

2 Put 2 biscuits into the air fryer and top each with 2 chocolate squares and 1 marshmallow. Put the other biscuits on top.

3 Cook for 2 minutes, until the chocolate and marshmallows have melted.

Doughnuts

Pillowy, soft and crisp on the outside, these doughnuts could be stuffed with jam or custard, depending on your mood.

120ml (4½fl oz) milk
45g (1¾oz) butter
7g (¼oz) sachet of
   fast-action dried yeast
4 tablespoons caster
   (superfine) sugar
1 teaspoon vanilla paste
250g (9oz) plain (all-
   purpose) flour, plus
   extra for dusting
½ teaspoon fine salt
1 egg, lightly beaten
vegetable oil, for the
   bowl

TO GLAZE

200g (7oz) icing sugar

1 Melt the milk and butter together in a microwaveable bowl in the microwave until lukewarm. Sprinkle over the yeast, then add 1 teaspoon of the sugar, along with the vanilla paste. Mix and leave to stand for 5 minutes. Put the remaining sugar into a medium-sized bowl with the flour and salt.

2 Add the beaten egg to the milk mixture and pour into the bowl of dry ingredients. Start bringing the dough together with your hands and knead for around 8 minutes, until smooth and elastic. You can also do this in a stand mixer fitted with a dough hook, working the machine for around 5 minutes. Transfer to a large oiled bowl and cover. Leave in a warm spot for around 1 hour until doubled in size.

3 Lightly flour a work surface, tip the dough out and roll it out to a thickness of 2cm (¾ inch). Using an 8cm (3¼ inch) round cutter, cut out 6 doughnuts, then use a 2cm (¾ inch) cutter to stamp out the middle holes (you may have to re-roll the dough offcuts to cut out all 6). Transfer the doughnuts to a baking tray lined with baking parchment, then cover and leave to prove for 30 minutes.

4 Preheat the air fryer to 180°C (350°F) for 4 minutes. Line the air fryer with an air fryer liner or baking parchment (parchment paper) that has been pierced with holes, then add the doughnuts. Cook for around 6 minutes. You may need to work in batches.

5 Meanwhile, sift the icing sugar into a medium-sized bowl. Whisk in 2 tablespoons of cold water until you have a thick, runny mix.

6 When the doughnuts come out of the air fryer, leave to cool on a wire rack for a few minutes. Then, dip the top of each doughnut into the icing to coat, and serve.

Brownies

Making brownies in an air fryer couldn't be easier. You'll need a tray that fits inside your basket. Incredibly rich and fudgy, these are so quick to whip up that you'll be making them all the time.

35g (1¼oz) vegetable oil, plus more for the tin

120g (4¼oz) caster (superfine) sugar

50g (1¾oz) plain (all-purpose) flour

35g (1¼oz) unsweetened cocoa powder

¼ teaspoon fine salt

1 egg

½ teaspoon vanilla paste

45g (1¾oz) dark chocolate nibs

1 Oil a 19cm (7½ inch) tin and line it with baking parchment (parchment paper).

2 In a medium-sized bowl, mix together the sugar, flour, cocoa powder and salt.

3 Pour the oil into a measuring jug and add the egg, vanilla paste and 1 tablespoon of cold water, then whisk.

4 Preheat the air fryer to 140°C (275°F) for 4 minutes.

5 Pour the wet ingredients into the bowl of dry ingredients and whisk until smooth, then fold in the chocolate nibs. Spread out the batter in the prepared tin and cook for 25 minutes.

6 Leave to cool for 5 minutes, then remove from the tin and place on a wire rack to cool completely.

Basque Cheesecake

This traditional Spanish cheesecake uses quite a different cooking method to other cheesecakes: you intentionally burn the top, yet retain a wobbly centre. It gives a wonderful caramelised taste and unmistakable texture.

butter or oil, for the tin
400g (14oz) full-fat cream cheese
110g (4oz) caster (superfine) sugar
1 tablespoon plain (all-purpose) flour
100g (3½oz) soured cream
2 eggs
2 teaspoons vanilla extract

1 Butter or oil a round tin that fits into the air fryer, about 19cm (7½ inches) in diameter, then line it with baking parchment (parchment paper). Preheat the air fryer to 190°C (375°F) for 4 minutes.

2 Put the cream cheese into a medium-sized bowl with the sugar, then, using electric beaters, whisk for 1 minute.

3 Add the flour, soured cream, eggs and vanilla extract, then whisk until smooth.

4 Tip into the prepared tin and cook for 30 minutes. The cheesecake should be dark on top with a slight wobble.

5 Leave to cool for at least 30 minutes before serving.

Apple Turnovers

These feel like a fast-food indulgence. Try swapping cinnamon for cardamom for an aromatic change.

2 Bramley (cooker) apples, peeled, cored and cut into 2cm (¾ inch) chunks

2 tablespoons light brown soft sugar

1 teaspoon ground cinnamon

juice of ½ lemon

1 × 320g (11½oz) sheet of ready-rolled puff pastry

1 egg, lightly beaten

2 tablespoons demerara (turbinado) sugar

1 In a medium-sized bowl, mix together the apple chunks, brown sugar, cinnamon and lemon juice.

2 Unroll the pastry sheet and cut into 4 equal rectangles. Add some of the apple filling to one half of each rectangle, then fold the opposite half over and crimp the edges with a fork.

3 Preheat the air fryer to 190°C (375°F) for 4 minutes. Brush the turnovers with the beaten egg and sprinkle over the demerara sugar.

4 Put the turnovers into the air fryer and cook for 8 minutes, until puffed up and golden.

Salted Caramel Cupcakes

You'll need a small cupcake tray to make these, but it's worth the investment: the batter comes together so quickly, and you could easily top them with buttercream frosting, or a light spreading of mascarpone for a sweet-and-savoury vibe.

50g (1¾oz) caster (superfine) sugar
50g (1¾oz) butter, softened
1 egg
1 teaspoon vanilla extract
1 tablespoon milk
50g (1¾oz) self-raising (self-rising) flour
3 teaspoons shop-bought salted caramel sauce, plus extra for drizzling

1 Put the sugar and butter into a medium-sized bowl and whisk with electric beaters until pale and fluffy. Add the egg, vanilla extract and milk, then whisk again until smooth. Fold in the flour until combined.

2 Preheat the air fryer to 150°C (300°F) for 4 minutes.

3 Line a 6-hole cupcake tin with cupcake cases. Fill each case halfway with the batter, then distribute the caramel sauce between the cupcakes. Top with the remaining batter.

4 Place the tin into the air fryer and cook for 15 minutes, until golden and risen.

5 Place on a wire rack to cool completely, then drizzle with more caramel sauce and serve.

Index